WHEN WE WERE
THIN

MUSIC, MADNESS AND MANCHESTER

Alberto Y Lost Trios Paranoias

AB

WHEN WE WERE
THIN

MUSIC, MADNESS AND MANCHESTER

Alberto Y Lost Trios Paranoias

CP LEE

Hotun Press

FIRST PUBLISHED IN GREAT BRITAIN IN 2007 BY

Hotun Press

www.itsahotun.com

COPYRIGHT © CP LEE 2007

CP Lee has asserted his right under the copyright, designs and patents act 1988 to be identified as the author of this work

Printed in the UK by Lightning Source UK Ltd

All rights reserved. No part of this publication may be reproduced, stored in the retrieval system or transmitted in any form or by any means, electronic, mechanical, photocopying, recording or otherwise, without the prior permission in writing of the author.

ISBN 978-0-9556257-0-1

ACKNOWLEDGEMENTS

This book would not have been possible but for the following:

THE ENTIRE ALBERTOS AND CREW

THE ENTIRE BLACKHILL ENTERPRISES

PAM LEE

SEAN BODY

GRAPHIC DESIGN

NICK JACKSON

PHOTO CREDITS

AB	ADRIAN BOOT
BW	BERNIE WILCOX
GM	GED MURRAY
JH	JIMMY HINDS
JB	JUNE BUCHAN
MM	MARK MAKIN
P	PRIVATE
RT	RUSS TARLOW

Every effort has been made to contact the copyright holders of the images in this book, but some proved untraceable. The copyright holders should contact the publishers for crediting in any future editions.

WHEN WE WERE THIN

MUSIC, MADNESS AND MANCHESTER

Alberto Y Lost Trios Paranoias

FORE FOREWORD BY DIMITRI GRILIOPOULOS		viii-ix
FOREWORD BY JIMMY HIBBERT		x-xii
DRAMATIS PERSONAE		xiii-xvi

CHAPTER 1	HOW IT ALL DONE COME TO BE	1
CHAPTER 2	WHEN THE MODE OF THE MUSIC CHANGES	13
CHAPTER 3	THE BIRTH OF THE BERTS	33
CHAPTER 4	HALF MAN HALF VAN - THE ROCKY ROAD TO?	51
CHAPTER 5	CARVING A CAREER IN ROCK	71
CHAPTER 6	PLAYING FOR THE STONED HEADS OF EUROPE	91
CHAPTER 7	FIXTURES, FORCES AND FRIENDS	117
CHAPTER 8	SLEAK: A FUN SHOW ABOUT DEATH	141
CHAPTER 9	IN THE PAW OF THE PIG	159
CHAPTER 10	GUERILLAS IN THE MIST	187
CHAPTER 11	THE CURSE OF THE BERTS	205

FORE FOREWORD

Dimitri Griliopoulos

AB

Hmm the Berts ...

I first saw them sometime in the 1970s at the old Manchester Polytechnic performing one of their sharp, witty, polished, slick, sick, and yes sleakly prickly yet professional routines involving music and humour - for that is what they did (sometimes). At other times they had their heads - like Lenny Bruce's Flamenco dancer - so firmly up their backsides it was hard to comprehend just what they were on about. Audiences however still smiled politely and gave them the clap they so richly deserved (another example of their 'wit').

Having performed at the same venue a few weeks before with Drive In Rock - a spoof 1950s Rock 'n' Roll 12 piece - and witnessed our gig end in a major brawl with our lead singer the late, lamented and nearly always out of tune Leroy Kool almost kicked to death on the floor by a gang of Teddy boys, I felt it might be time for a change. I don't think the men in drapes and funny shoes liked seeing their beloved R&R having the piss taken out of it by a bunch of obvious acid wrecked dope smoking hippies doo-wopping wildly. So I hung up my bass to dry and signed on as Roadie, Helper, Friend with ambulance, PA and mongrel Jeremy. We - the boys (for they were still in their short pants) and I then spent many months, nay years, trailing the highways of Euroland in search of fame and fortune. But the Rainbow kept shifting, and that pot of gold just kept one step ahead.

Most of us are born young, but Les always had to be a bit different. I knew he was dying - so did he, somehow we could cope with that. But after Ray left the band incomprehensibly (you couldn't understand a word he was saying so scrambled was he) and sweet Jeremy bolted from the Marquee Club dressing room one night (I spent the whole knight walking Soho whistling and shouting 'JEREMY!' - and I didn't get arrested, or propositioned, or ever find him) I, like my little dog, had had enough. I even fell asleep, head on the mixing desk, at one gig in Gronigen and no one noticed that the knobs hadn't been twiddled once during the whole performance. I needed a change. I hung up my jangly keys one last time and signed off from the Berts.

I bought some long bendy trucks and for some years transferred larger and larger lorry loads of amplifiers and speakers around Europe, whilst the Albertos continued peddling their tripe and onions wherever they could. They invented public hanging well before YouTube, taking their Snuff Rock classic Sleak to at least two major continents. They continued kicking against the pricks (as St Paul said) - Richard Milhous Nixon being one of their main pissing posts, and if they were still treading the boards today I feel sure there would have been rubber Billy Liar of Downing Street and Sadly Insane of Iraq masks in their box of props. They were not just a cross between the Marx Brothers and the Barron Knights, they could be quite nasty if they saw a prick that needed kicking. In fact they weren't anything like a cross between the Marx Brothers and the Barron Knights - well, maybe just a bit. They came, and they went. Frankly I was glad to see the back of them. Their front - I didn't mind, but their back.

I give you - Alberto Y Lost Trios Paranoias! Take them away ... and don't bring them back!

I thank you!

Dimitri Griliopoulos
Kissoff De'ath Suite, Waldorf Towers, NY
April 2007

FOREWORD
Jimmy Hibbert

> We knew Lenny Bruce died in a toilet ...
> We didn't think we'd end up playing in it.

AB

... Amsterdam. On the way to the Melkweg in our trusty VW camper - trusty in the sense that it could be relied upon to explode at regular intervals. One engine blew up on the road between Rotterdam and Amsterdam, another on the M10 (where Ray had once, to the accompaniment of screams from the back seats, pulled a U-ey when he realised he was taking us in the wrong direction) and a third contrived to lose the use of one of its cylinders in Munich. The drive from beautiful Bavaria to Ostend was completed in 11 hours (non stop). We had a ferry to catch and the bus couldn't do more than 50mph on its three remaining cylinders.

As I was saying. Amsterdam. It's not an easy city to drive in. An awful lot of bicycles and many of the streets are (in the words of Robert Benchley - though he was in Venice at the time) filled with water. Bruce was at the wheel. He took a wrong turning and we found ourselves (as on the M10) travelling in the wrong direction – this time down a one way street. Cyclists hurled themselves out of the way of the oncoming Bertmobile. Other vehicles were forced on to the pavement. Pedestrians shouted and swore at us. It was a policeman who managed to stop the determined Mitchell by bravely standing in front of the bus and holding up an admonishing hand. Bruce wound down the window and smiled a disarming smile that could have turned milk into yoghurt at thirty yards.

"It's all right, officer" he said by way of explanation and expiation, "We're a group."

And indeed we were. As disparate a group of people as were ever crammed into an orange and cream VW camper van. So it was that I, public school educated and armed with an extremely good third class degree in Drama (I might have fared better had Manchester University offered a course in spliff rolling - I could have managed a first in that) found myself rubbing shoulders and larking about on stages as far apart as Aberdeen and Tel Aviv with the likes of the other Berts; Berts such as Bob 'Bob' Harding, who would only consider having a goldfish as a pet as all other animals whined for food and attention. But he did sport the best haircut in the band when he had it cropped shortish and dyed a sort of purpley colour.

Prize for worst hair went, not to me - though I admit mine was pretty unfashionable by the time punk arrived, hair went all spiky, mohican and green and I stuck to my old quasi-hippy long and shaggy look - but to Les Prior, whose haphazardly cut and dyed hair sometimes looked like the pelt of a drug-addled hamster who had died from a severe case of St. Vitus' dance. As for his dental organisation, that made Shane MacGowan look like Richard Branson.

Ray Hughes was also a trifle deficient in the gnasher department, though he did have a set of false ones to fill the gaps. These were occasionally removed when the Welsh muse came upon him and he wanted to add a bit of gummy colour to his incomprehensible declamations.

The only thing more incomprehensible than Ray's Welsh outpourings was Dimitri's laugh. Like a cross between a pig eating its own tail and a drain being scoured for a set of lost keys, the strange and raucous braying would drown out any more conventional laughter between mixing desk and stage. He even hee-hawed when a dubious choice of paramour-for-the-evening managed to spill her tequila sunrise all over the important bits of the desk one night at the Marquee Club. The resultant noise from the speakers was sufficient to drown out that made by the near-hysterical Dimitri.

Tony Bowers. One of the sunniest of people from midday until bedtime. Impossible in the mornings. He once asked me to wake him at nine. I did. I was subjected to a torrent of abuse, so I reminded him that he'd actually asked me to wake him. "WELL, I'M AWAKE, AREN'T I?!?"
Simon 'Tommy' White, a product, like me, of the public school system, spent a lot of time snoozing in the back of the van, as we covered mile after mile en route to the next gig, with a book in his hand and his finger on the word he'd reached as sleep overtook him. Once he awoke he'd continue to read from the point where he left off. And I defy anyone in the world to give a more raucous rendition of the theme tune to *The Archers* on a Fender Stratocaster than he.

Bruce's passport sported a sort of 'before' and 'after' picture. In those days, the holder could renew a passport every ten years simply by adding a more recent photograph. The "before" picture showed Bruce as a somewhat younger man, in suit and tie, and with a sensible short haircut. The "after" was the Bruce we knew. This Bruce grinned from the passport like a mutant orang-utan on acid, his hair shoulder-length and slightly unkempt, and sporting a couple of oil-smudges from a bike he might recently have acquired. It was this that confused an East German border guard when our passports were shot down to him along a passport pipeline from one bunker to the next. He called out our names as he examined the photos before handing back our passports. When he came to Bruce's, his face, formerly so stern and unforgiving, took on an expression approaching sympathy. He was under the impression that the passport was held by husband and wife – the wife being the "after" picture.

Then there were the diminutive Chris Wainwright, the unfortunate Dave Caspar; and latterly John Scott, as talented with guitar and saxophone as he was at making the contents of a beer bottle disappear; and Captain Mog, who blinked a lot.

Oh, and C.P. I first met CP in 1972 when I was drafted in to work (well, laze about behind the incense and hippy trinket counter) at the infamous Manchester hippy emporium 'On the Eighth Day'. He was, without doubt - and believe me, I'd met some pretty weird types since I'd exchanged the sanity and sobriety of the Home Counties for mad Manchester - the funniest, maddest, bonkersest person I'd ever come across. By turns affable and infuriating, generous and self-seeking, loveable and exasperating, hilarious and dour, he was, in the words of my grandmother, quite biffy.

Nothing that has happened in the intervening thirty-five years has done anything to alter my first impressions. And don't let the following pages of sane and thoughtful analysis, comment and reminiscence allow you, dear reader, to believe anything else.

DRAMATIS PERSONAE

Over the course of roughly ten years Alberto Y Lost Trios Paranoias directly changed the lives of thousands of people with their unique blend of biting satire and car repair manuals. It would be impossible to list them here, so this is restricted to people who either played with, worked for or somehow lived with the Albertos. There are doubtless many more who should be included here, but they're not in this book - so tough.

Musicians - alphabetical first name

Bob Harding
Founder member of AYLTP, with Jimmy Hibbert and CP Lee. Left due to 'musical indifference' and eventually founded 'Blood and Fire' Records.

Bruce Mitchell
Long-term Mancunian musician. With the Albertos from their inception to their demise. Now with the Durutti Column.

Captain Mog
Started as bass player for The Smirks, before joining the Berts. A brief spell on TV soap Brookside after his discharge papers came through, now ALL Radio DJ and gigging with The Lonesome & Penniless Cowboys.

Chris Wainwright
Original guitarist with the band. Resigned on a point of principle as we were about to embark on our conquest of Europe. Entered politics.

CP Lee
Eminence gris behind the Berts. After that, wrote for TV and stage before giving it all up to become an academic. Now eminence gris of the Salford Sheiks.

Dave Casper
Original bass player with the Albertos from our early musical experiments at the Squat. Appallingly 'dumped' by the band shortly after we signed with Blackhill Enterprises in 1974. Took up religion.

Jimmy Hibbert
Founder member of AYLTP, now a highly successful 'voice over' artist for TV and radio.

John Scott
Highly talented multi-instrumentalist. Worked with Martin Hannett and John Cooper Clarke at Rabid Records and put out pet projects on Absurd Records. Still playing.

Les Prior
Factor 'X' – Insane luminary with whom it was a joy to share the planet and all. Les worked not only with the Berts, but also acted as MC for Stiff Record tours. Died from cancer, 1980. His funeral was one of the best gigs I've ever been to.

Ray 'Mongo' Hughes
Wonderfully eccentric drummer who joined the band as a 'replacement' for Bruce. One night at the Nashville Rooms in London he accidentally drank a pint of piss. Left due to ill-health, became carpenter and free-jazz drummer. Died 2006, RIP

Simon 'Tommy' White
Guitarist extraordinaire, almost from the band's beginning, all the way to the bitter end, Simon was a uniquely eccentric character, but not as eccentric as his grandparents. Eventually got a proper job.

Tony Bowers
Bass and lead guitar till 1978 when he went off with Bob Harding and formed the short-lived 'Mothmen' which sort of mutated into 'Simply Red'. Married an Italian mud-wrestler.

Others - alphabetical first name

Andrew King
Co-founder of Blackhill Enterprises who managed, amongst others, Syd Barrett and The Pink Floyd, Marc Bolan and T Rex, Kevin Ayers and the Whole World, Pete Brown and Piblokto, The Third Ear Band, Roy Harper, The Edgar Broughton Band and Alberto Y Lost Trios Paranoias. Now heads Mute Music publishing company. Handled the Albertos day-to-day affairs.

Anthony Wilson
Journalist, TV presenter and early champion of the Albertos. He went on to found Factory Records and opened the world-famous Hacienda Club. Still highly influential and controversial. Died 10 August 2007, RIP.

Arthur Kelly
Mate of George Harrison's who played opposite Gorden Kaye in Sleak.

Black Paul Young
A native of St Lucia in the West Indies, Black Paul was a popular figure on the Manchester roady circuit. He worked with the Albertos for several years before becoming 'head-humper' at the Apollo Theatre. Our secret weapon against the Pink Floyd. Died in 1996.

Charlie Hanson
Director of Sleak, and director of the Black Theatre Workshop. Now works in TV as a producer.

Claude Bessey
Anarchic French bohemian. Co-founder of Slash Magazine in LA, which he wrote for under the name 'Kick-Boy Face'. Featured in Penelope Spheeris' film *The Decline of Western Civilisation*. Came to England in 1982 to work as video jockey at the Haçienda. Died in Barcelona, 1999, RIP.

Dimitri Griliopoulis
Former member of Drive In Rock who became the Albertos' first roady because he had an old ambulance and a PA. Eventually went on to open 'Dimitri's' chain of bars and restaurants.

Dougie Marnoch
A mainstay of the Alberto road crew for many years, Doug still 'treads the boards' for those that beckon. Unwittingly one of the inspirations for *Sleak*, the Albertos' highly acclaimed stage show.

Dutch Jan
An overseas import to the Alberto camp, Jan arrived back in England with them after a particularly strenuous tour of the Netherlands when they discovered that his powerful physique enabled him to lift lots of stuff their roadies wouldn't touch. Eventually returned to Holland and is missed.

Elliott Rashman
A former student who was taken on as an Alberto roady, he quickly learned the lessons of 'dynamic management' from Andrew King and went on to guide the careers of Mick Hucknall and Simply Red.

Gorden Kaye
Jobbing actor who joined the Albertos as Jack Plugg in their successful stage show Sleak. Ignoring all their advice he accepted the lead role in a TV series called 'Ello 'Ello and went on to international stardom.

Harry Demac
Owner, operator of a PA hire firm, Harry fitted in perfectly with the laissez faire attitude of the Albertos. His diminutive style leant itself superbly to tasteless gags and much ribbing. Still at it. Master of his own destiny.

Judy Lloyd
Played the part of Sandra in the London and European production of Sleak. Had to wear 'funny' clothes.

Lawrence Beadle
Confidante and assistant to Tosh Ryan at Rabid Records before founding Absurd Records. Absurd produced a bunch of eccentric singles that utilised several Albertos, including Captain Mog, John Scott and CP Lee. Gave up the music business and is now involved in local politics.

Martin Hannett
Internationally renowned music producer. Tosh Ryan's partner at Rabid before moving on to Factory Records where he was house producer, creating the unique studio sounds for artists such as New Order and Durutti Column before falling foul of the evil fruit of the poppy. He died in 1991, RIP.

Mike Clement
From student archaelogist to internationally renowned guitar tech via the Berts university of roadydom.

Penny and Tessa
The Albertos were striking a blow for sexual equality when these two women joined their road crew, and the Berts were really boxing clever because they were the best in the country at their particular jobs.

Peter Jenner
Other half of Blackhill Enterprises with Andrew King. Acted principally as record producer for the Albertos. Now manages Billy Bragg.

Richard Boon
Manager of Buzzcocks from 1977 till 1981. Founder of New Hormones record label. Went on to Rough Trade Records and The Cartel, where he worked closely with the Smiths and KLF. Now a librarian in London.

Roger Eagle
Larger than life figure, influential in so many musical fields. 'Invented' Northern Soul at the world famous Twisted Wheel Club in Manchester in the early 1960s. Manager of Greasy Bear, manager of Liverpool Eric's Club and The International in Manchester. Mentor and friend to countless musicians including Mick Hucknall, CP Lee, Echo and The Bunnymen and many more. Died 4th May 1999, RIP

Tosh Ryan
Legendary Manchester saxophonist who worked with Victor Brox amongst others. One of the mainstays of musicians' co-operative Music Force before founding Rabid Records with Martin Hannett. Became a multi-media arts facilitator/archivist. Never sartorially challenged.

CHAPTER ONE

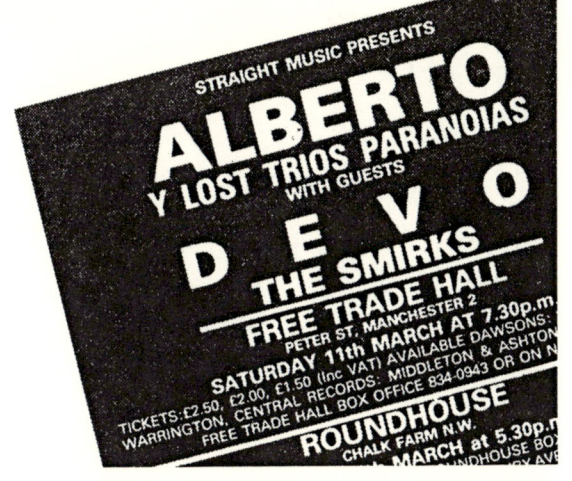

1

HOW IT ALL DONE COME TO BE

STRAIGHT MUSIC PRESENTS

ALBERTO
Y LOST TRIOS PARANOIAS
WITH GUESTS

D E V O
THE SMIRKS

FREE TRADE HALL
PETER ST, MANCHESTER 2
SATURDAY 11th MARCH AT 7.30p.m
TICKETS: £2.50, £2.00, £1.50 (inc VAT) AVAILABLE DAWSONS:
WARRINGTON, CENTRAL RECORDS: MIDDLETON & ASHTON
FREE TRADE HALL BOX OFFICE 834-0943 OR ON N

ROUNDHOUSE
CHALK FARM N.W.
MARCH at 5.30p.m

Manchester had slumbered on through the Forties and Fifties with the combined effects of the Second World War, its rationing and early closing in pubs, in much the same way as the rest of the monochrome isles. Likewise when Hedonism in the 1960s crept up on Great Britain, nothing was done about the great slobbering beast that, as a hungry lion successfully stalks its prey, took a hold of the Great British Culture. Little could be done except to watch its children run wild through paisley-coloured fields, seduced by the drumbeat of modern music. By the early 1960s Manchester was home to dozens of Jazz, Folk and Beat Clubs, havens of retreat for kids bored with and disrespectful of the post-war sterility and austerity, and fuelled by the jingling in their pockets of economic freedom they were ready to make a new reality.

I was born at the beginning of 1950, exactly half way through the last century. By 1964 I was just a couple of years out of the TB sanatorium, ashamed of my fat body, and obsessed with Airfix plastic aeroplane kits. I watched Pop musicians on the TV with undiluted scorn, yet glowed with pride when my Aunty Pat handed me a copy of Freddie and The Dreamers' first LP as a Christmas present. It had been signed by the group! The drummer, Bernie Dwyer was my second cousin (so too was Morrissey I was to find out years later) and, at last, I thought I could hold my head up at school because I had a bona-fide connection to the rapidly growing world of Pop. Now maybe girls would like me! But as a passport to sexual pleasure (which I had a vague inkling about, if no specific idea or knowledge thereof), I didn't find such a connection any use. My score in hipness was probably not helped either by my insistence on dressing like my father in tweed jacket, cavalry twill trousers and a cravat, while all my contemporaries were wearing Chelsea boots and Beatle jackets.

Of course I would try to get switched on by *Top of the Pops* and *Thank Your Lucky Stars* - how much easier it would be to connect with the crowd if I were to, but much of it didn't work for me at all. I'd been brought up to the sound of my mother's voice singing me songs about fishermen and gypsies and soldiers who went wooing. Later, from our radiogram that we had installed in the late 1950s, my mother would play Josh White and Big Bill Broonzy LPs. So, whilst my friends' mothers were playing their albums of *My Fair Lady* and *South Pacific* I was

P 1958 Preparing for the Cultural Revolution

picking up on the Blues and R 'n' B sounds that was emerging from the early Beat movement.

When our music teacher at school started giving us lessons on Folk music, I was hooked. I don't know his name. He only lasted a year and then had a breakdown, or so I'm told, but I'm grateful to him still, and I don't imagine his breakdown was other than personal to him as our school was not a particularly hard one in terms of pupil/teacher relationships. Named the High School of Art it had been founded as a bold experiment after the war by the Manchester Education Committee and its pupils were fed through by the Headteachers of all Manchester's primary schools who would seek out those children with keen artistic talent.

Something to sing

COMPILED BY GEOFFREY BRACE

MELODY EDITION

CAMBRIDGE · AT THE UNIVERSITY PRESS · 1963

My actual school song book

The pupils at the High School of Art were pulled out of the mainstream at the age of eleven and their studies were concentrated in drawing, painting, pottery and sculpture classes all of which took the more prominent position in the school's curriculum. John Mayall had gone there before conscription and the Korean War had carried him off in another direction. Purposefully we were made aware that we were being hot-housed and destined for the rapidly expanding Art schools of England. We knew that Hornsey, Chelsea and St Martin's beckoned ... but then there was the Folk music ...

So this music teacher, a big bear of a man with a beard, but ever such a gentle voice, had veered away radically from the syllabus and soon stopped trying to get the class to sing such choral delights as *Where The Bee Sups There Sup I*, and a German song called something like *Der Ist Ein Rose Ensprungen*, by playing LPs of people like Pete Seeger and getting us to sing along from a publication entitled, *Something To Sing*.

This book, which I still possess (sorry school library), had songs in it like *Jesse James*, *The Greenland Whale Fisheries* and Ewan MacColl's *Dirty Old Town*. Whenever I listen to The Pogue's first album I'm convinced Shane McGowan had the same songbook at his school. One day I inherited from one of my elder brothers a Dansette C30 portable record player and was able to borrow the school's Folk albums and take them home to listen to in the privacy of my own bedroom (these I gave back, library).

From the music classes at school to the public face of the Folk Revival and the couple of TV shows that it engendered, I found I had a musical identity at last or at least a direction to focus on. In my bedroom, surrounded by plastic models of Dornier and Heinkel bombers, I would sing along to numbers like *The Titanic*, *Pretty Polly* and the haunting *Willie Moore*.

By the fourth year at school I fell in love with a willowy blonde called Denise who was in the sixth form. She wore a duffel coat and a CND badge. She appeared to my eyes to be tremendously sophisticated. I wore a blue raincoat and a blue alpine hat with a feather in it. Occasionally I sported a pipe to make myself look more mature than my fourteen years of age. I hoped to her eyes I might appear also sophisticated and I was encouraged to discover that she went to Folk clubs. Surely the Gods had contrived to bring us together. I began to make enquiries as to which clubs she frequented. My secret plan to win her over was to suddenly appear in front of her at one of these gigs and say something like, "Oh, Denise. What a surprise. Did you know I'm singing here tonight?" so obviously, my secret plan involved me somehow becoming a Folk singer.

"There's two things a fella can do, boy – One is to sing, the other is play the guitar – If I were you, I'd stick to singin'"
Spider John Koerner to CP Lee, 1964.

Faint heart n'er won fair lady, so of course I had to ask around, to casually enquire where Denise went to listen to Folk music. I was quite astonished to find out that she attended a club in Fallowfield fairly near to where I lived. The obvious disadvantage to meeting up with her there was my age, but with my steely resolve and the cunning deployment of my pipe, I might pass for sixteen. Actually, as I mentioned earlier, I was a big bugger and had begun shaving at thirteen, Hell, I could pass for eighteen given a dark night and a judicious application of Old Spice aftershave to add a veneer of maturity.

The next step was to create a repertoire of songs. I'd read in a local Folk rag that the only true Folk singing was done unaccompanied, so not having an instrument, let alone not being able to play one was no problem. I would rely on my voice. The purchase of an Alex Campbell live LP in Woolworth's bargain range had resulted in the addition of several new songs to my roster – *The Bonnie Ship The Diamond* and *The Barnyards of Delgathay*. Wherever Alex had an instrumental break in his songs I'd simply leave a gap. God, it was all so simple!

I tried to press several chums into coming with me. David MacMullen lived too far away in North Manchester and David Brooks saw through my cunning plan for the farrago of flatulence it really was and wisely wanted nothing to do with it. So, one wet and windy night in the late autumn of 1964, I told my parents I was going to visit friends and walked alone from Didsbury to Fallowfield. I climbed up the steps of an old Victorian mansion that housed the Fallowfield Folk Club and went inside.

A beatnik-type fellow (who I'd later come to know very well) sat at a desk by the door. I could tell he was a beatnik because he had a goatee beard and was wearing tinted glasses, all of which I took to be very racy. After barely glancing up he said, "That'll be 1/6d, mate". He took my money and I entered into the thrilling environs of the Fallowfield Conservative Club, which was, for some bizarre reason, home to this bastion of radicalism. A hand-written sign said 'Folk Club In Cellar', with an arrow pointing down. There was the noise of a bar to my left.

I went in and faced my first proper challenge of the night, possibly of my life up to that point. Stood behind the bar was a blue-rinsed-hair-doed-woman, seemingly distracted by boredom, who asked me, "What would you like to drink, love?" Fearful that I was about to fail the whole ruse because I had no idea of what I'd like to drink and I'd never even been inside a pub before in my life and had absolutely no idea of what to order, I went red-faced and felt dizzy. It seemed the whole bar had gone quiet and that everybody was looking at me. I remained steadfastly tongue-tied.

"Yes, love", she asked again, more impatiently, definitely it seemed with loud interest. I ran through my memory banks and came up with a drink that I'd heard ordered on *Coronation Street* on the TV.

"A milk stout please", I answered, inwardly heaving a sigh of relief.

"We don't sell that love."

"Shit!"

"Erm, er, a brown ale please", I managed to reply with the name of another beer from the "Street'.

Reaching under the bar she pulled out a bottle of brown ale, blew the dust off the cap and opened it. Pouring it into a glass she said, "That'll be tenpence please, love".

1964 Cambridge with Dad (note sullen pose)

Christ! Tenpence! This was proving to be an expensive night out, and I'd only been in the building five minutes. Pressing on anyway and jauntily cocking my alpine hat with a feather, onto the back of my head, and with glass of ale in hand, I strode manfully down into the cellar to make my world debut on the stage. After negotiating a particularly narrow set of stairs I came into the bit of the basement where performances took place. About twenty feet long it had eight or nine rows of benches facing what looked essentially like a space on the floor. Indeed, it was a space on the floor. The phrase 'floor singers' which I'd read about in Folk magazines now took on a more literal meaning. Half a dozen or so members of the audience were dotted hither and yon around the space and in that one scope I could see, Denise wasn't amongst them.

It was time to take stock, to appraise myself of the situation. At present nothing seemed to be happening, just a quiet murmur as one or two of the audience talked to each other. I took a seat on one of the benches about mid-way down the room and began to wonder if this was such a good idea. I tried to mentally go through my set, but my mind had gone blank. As I pathetically tried to recall the opening lines of any of the numbers that I knew, a voice from behind stirred me from my reverie.

"Dylan is a bastard! He's a stinking sell-out bastard!" An intense young man with a guitar case, entering the cellar, was proclaiming loudly to another young man as they walked to the front. I'd seldom seen such passion roused in anybody. Their conversation continued, "Ah, come on man – he's a great song writer", exclaimed the second young man. "He was!" interrupted the first guy excitedly. "Until he went commercial! – look, Folk doesn't sell out to the top ten, and that's all he's doing on his new album – writing shit for tin-pan alley. If he wants to be in the top ten, all very well and good for him, but he doesn't have to drag us there with him! He's sold out!"

I forgot about my set problem. Who was this Dylan they were talking about?

The beatnik from upstairs strode into the cellar and stalked to the performance area and the Dylan argument could continue no further as he began speaking –

"Good evening ladies and gentlemen, and welcome to the Fallowfield Folk Club. We'll start in a couple of minutes with a set from an old friend of ours, Ted Jones, then it's open floor time with anybody who feels like getting up and singing. After that, we'll have an intermission and then Barry and Les will be inviting us to join in on some shanties before our main guest of the evening, Ryan Roberts."

Before he had a chance to step down, the young guy shouted at him –

"What do you think of Dylan, Paul?"

"I think he's great" replied the MC, club organiser, whatever, I wasn't sure what he was, at that stage, but he seemed to be running things.

"Bollocks!" Came another voice. "He's shite! Totally sold out!"

"Ladies and gentlemen, Ted Jones", responded 'Paul' and the young guy who'd come in arguing took to the 'stage'.

A smattering of applause and he unpacked his guitar and started tuning it. Then he introduced his first song, The Dirty Black Leg Miner, which he explained was about 'scabs', 'those bastards who'd sell out their own kith and kin' while their fellow miners were on strike. He sang it with gusto and I warmed to him. Then he sang a song about the Irish Republican Army and everyone laughed. Finally he sang about 'little washer lads' working for 'fourpence a day' and he had me totally won over.

The space had filled up quite a lot by then and I noticed with a quickening of the heart, there was Denise. Sat at the back with a group of girl friends. I decided to play it cool by remaining totally motionless with fear.

Paul came back on as Ted returned to the benches and announced that now was open floor time and would anybody like to get up and sing. I sat quietly, basically hoping that nobody had noticed me. Nobody spoke, so Paul spoke for us –

"How about you, sir? Would you like to get up and give us a song? Ladies and gentlemen, a new face amongst us tonight. Would you care to sing us a song?"

The growing realisation that I was the object of his introduction was fettling over me like a storm cloud. I looked round at him and I automatically stood up, as if in a dream but feeling like it was a nightmare. If I didn't sing I'd look like an idiot, and if I did sing, I'd be a complete idiot.

Then suddenly it was me, this complete idiot who stumbled towards the 'stage' area and blinked out over the eight or nine rows of benches to find that enough people to fill Maine Road Football Ground were all staring expectantly. I undid my raincoat and as I did so I remember I shot a glance over at Denise who was, given the circumstances looking rather more puzzled than shocked.

How It All Done Come To Be 9

"And what's your name?" asked Paul.

"Chris Lee," I answered.

"Ladies and gentlemen, our first floor singer for this evening - Chris Lee"

I began very well - "Thank you" - I said. My brain rushed through the key-words section and then came up with –

"I'd like to do a Traditional song by, er, well, it's Traditional, so it isn't by anybody that I know of and tonight I'd like to do it by myself, thank you, it was written by the 19th century."

I then lurched into an indefensible version of *Turpin Hero* stolen from *Something To Sing*, that was marred only by the fact that after the first line, 'As Turpin rode across the moor' my mouth completely dried up and I had to sing the rest of the song in a variety of bewilderingly different keys in order to accommodate the varying circumstances of my mouth.

P 1967 The High School of Art up against the wall

"Not bad for a first ever gig," I remember thinking! To several bewildered looks and a faint smattering of polite applause my first ever gig had come to an end. And do you know what? I loved it. I lurched back to my seat and re-ran my performance through my head again and again while some pathetic no-hoper, amateur singer took the floor and sang some songs properly, but without, I felt, any emotional commitment. Then came the intermission and I stood up looking for Denise. To my surprise she was deep in conversation with Ted. They were holding albums and looking intensely at the covers. I wandered over as casually as I could manage.

"I didn't know you sang", she said. "Yeah, well, you know. I've always been into Folk," I replied.

"Right then. Give us your opinion of Dylan", snapped Ted. "You're obviously a Traditional singer. I can't see you having much time for him."

Never having heard of Dylan until that night when I'd walked into the club, I felt at some disadvantage, obviously, but I thought Ted's set had been really good, plus, he was older than me and therefore presumably knew what he was talking about. And in order to further impress Denise, it seemed a good idea to agree with the outburst I'd heard him give when he arrived in the cellar, "Well, he's obviously sold out. I mean, he was quite good once, but now... well, he's gone commercial, hasn't he?" I answered, waving my pipe about for authority.

"I totally disagree," said Denise looking a tad too feisty for my liking. "I think he's brilliant!"

What?!? This wasn't supposed to happen!

"What about *Times They Are A-Changin'*?" said Denise, testily.

"Oh well, that was a good one," answered Ted.

"Definitely." I added weakly.

"*Don't Think Twice*?" she snapped.

"I didn't." I defended myself.

"A great song, I'll admit, but what's it got to do with 'the people'?" argued Ted ignoring the idiocy of my comment, and putting an emphatic intonation on the word 'the people', that eluded me. "I don't think we'd find Chris singing it."

"Too commercial," I smiled vaguely, "but a very good song."

"Oh, you two are hopeless," shrugged Denise and went off to rejoin her friends.

And so it was that I became a part of the Manchester Folk scene and it didn't take me longer than 24 hours to track down somebody at school who owned a Dylan album. For a time I grappled with the dichotomy of the Folk scene, divided as it was in its two camps – the Traditionalists who saw themselves as defenders and propagators of some kind of 'People's Art', pure and aloof, untainted by commercial considerations - and the Modernists, for want of a better phrase, who were broadly eclectic in their tastes and seemed to me to be prepared to appreciate all different kinds of genres. As I immersed myself in a deep appreciation of Dylan, I soon became an enthusiastic flag bearer for the latter, with Dylan as my God and guide, I got myself a guitar and joined the queues at the Portland Street Music Exchange for the latest Whitmark and Sons' Bob Dylan songbooks. All within a couple of months of that first gig, I was practising avidly on my newly purchased guitar and I began appearing at least once a week on floor spots at a couple of clubs around town.

℗ 1966 St Ives, Cornwall. The Beat moves on ...

## CHAPTER TWO
WHEN THE MODE OF THE MUSIC CHANGES (THE WALLS OF THE CITY SHAKE)

STRAIGHT MUSIC PRESENTS

ALBERTO Y LOST TRIOS PARANOIAS
WITH GUESTS
DEVO
THE SMIRKS

FREE TRADE HALL
PETER ST, MANCHESTER 2
SATURDAY 11th MARCH AT 7.30p.m.
TICKETS: £2.50, £2.00, £1.50 (inc VAT) AVAILABLE DAWSONS, WARRINGTON, CENTRAL RECORDS: MIDDLETON & ASHTON
FREE TRADE HALL BOX OFFICE 834-0943 OR ON N…

ROUNDHOUSE
CHALK FARM N.W.
MARCH at 5.30p.m.

I lost a lot of weight around that time and I ditched the cravat. I got a summer job in 1965 and the first thing I bought myself was a pair of jeans. My mother nearly had a breakdown when I wore them to go out in one evening. "They're for working in!" she sobbed. "You look so common!" My hair was beginning to grow but it was naturally curly in that curly way that whatever it just remains singularly a mass of curls. The fashion for young guys in Manchester was for mod hairstyles, à la The Small Faces, long at the sides and backcombed into a bouffant at the back - curly headed people need not apply. With the only Chart Buster with similar hair being Tom Jones who was considered a jerk, Bob Dylan's hairstyle came as a salvation to me – just grow it, man. You don't even have to comb it.

Before I go any further, you're probably wondering what ever happened between me and Denise? The answer is - nothing. She did what I began to notice throughout my life lots of women do - she went off with a bloke she professed to dislike, ie Ted. By the time I noticed, I was way too busy burning bridges to care anyway.

Pop music was gradually mutating into Rock and I began to visit Beat clubs with friends from school. My musical tastes broadened wider and wider. I began buying music papers and was really into watching *Ready Steady Go* every Friday evening. When 1966 dawned I was well on the path to perdition and damnation. I was taking in an awful lot of music, ranging from UK performers like The Who, The Action, The Move, The Small Faces, Zoot Money, Graham Bond, Annie Briggs, Martin Carthy and Dave Swarbrick, all the way to American legends such as Sonny Boy Williamson, Ike and Tina Turner, Lee Dorsey, Bobby Bland and many, many more. Then on May 17th 1966, I was there when ice clashed with fire at the Free Trade Hall, when Dylan 'went electric' in Manchester and that gig for me was the catalyst that sent me spinning into performance and artistic freefall because it was that night when I decided I had to get me an electric guitar.

I'd been doing the acoustic thing for long enough. Firstly solo, trying, and usually failing, to fingerpick through Folk standards like *Candy Man* and *Cocaine*. I operated under the youthful and rather naïve assumption that there was no reason why a person shouldn't be able to play just as well as the best. I gave no consideration to natural ability or the concept of practice. Then I found that it was much easier to strum and it was with a leaping heart I realised that some of the chords were actually getting in my way! If they were a bit awkward to reach, or my fingers couldn't shape them, I began to leave them out. This is still pretty much the way I play today - passably. I found my voice, as it were, singing harmony with a boy and girl from the Folk world, Andy and Claire, and for a couple of months we performed as, wait for it – The Shuttlers! How hip could a Folk name get? It was with them that I realised my real forte lay in singing, but I still felt uncomfortable without a guitar around my neck for me to hide behind. Then, as I veered more and more away from English material into the more exotic grazing lands of American Folk, I began playing in a duo with a very gifted guitarist from my school, Mike King.

Mike and I went to see Dylan together that May and we left the Free Trade Hall determined to put together a band as soon as we possibly could. An appearance on *Ready Steady Go* by the Paul Butterfield Blues Band, a few weeks later, just made it more urgent. Gee, Elvin Bishop and Mike Bloomfield both had Dylanesque Izro's (after: Israel - as the bushy, birds-nest hairstyle came to be called)! Another summer job meant that I could afford to buy an instrument and an amp. Mike and I had come to an agreement - I was going to be the main singer and he was going to play lead guitar, because he was actually very good at it and I wasn't. It didn't make any sense having two electric guitarists even if one of them was only passably useful, so I opted to switch to bass. It even looked easier, two less strings to muck about with. And so, in November 1966 we finally had a band, though of course we'd overlooked the obvious in that we didn't have a drummer, nor did we have a name, but we knew we had a band and nothing was going to stop us.

Culturally, big changes were afoot. There was a long article published in the *Sunday Times* colour magazine on the 'Heaven and Hell' drug, LSD; it was illustrated with photos of Ken Kesey and The Merry Pranksters and I learnt about how one single dose of the drug could take its victim to the ecstatic shores of Paradise, or into the maelstrom of Hell. It seemed like good odds to me and I began to make urgent enquiries as to where I could locate a 'sugar cube' of 'acid' in Manchester. Having been raised a Roman Catholic, an ecstatic vision of Paradise was high on my agenda of 'must sees'. Hell, on the other hand, was just around the corner to us poor miserable sinners anyway, so what the heck? Plus, it was legal!

Another thing at the time to fascinate me was a *World In Action* documentary on the burgeoning 'Underground' scene, and the newly emerging hippies. Strobe lights flickered and coloured blobs whirled round a room full of dancing teenagers who were wearing flowers in their hair and talking of poetry and metaphysics, peace and love. The scene seemed to evolve around California and surprisingly, London. Lots of new-style music was playing and soon *Melody Maker* began to review groups like the Mothers of Invention and our own home-grown Pink Floyd, so as 1966 turned into 1967, me and Mike were ready to dip our toes into the sea of chaos and see what colour they turned.

A mate of ours, Mike Reynolds had come up with a band's name for us - Jacko Ogg and The Head People - the off-set litho print room at school was busy churning out what we thought were pretty authentic looking psychedelic posters which we merrily stuck up all over town. We even had a drummer now, Pete, a friend of a friend of a friend, who had a kit because he played in the Boys Brigade. One of my art teachers, Miss Paterson let us rehearse in her loft around the corner from my house. Every Saturday we'd get together to work on the set. We did versions of Dylan's *Positively 4th Street*, and Just Like *Tom Thumb's Blues*, John Mayall's *Key To Love* and *Crocodile Blues*, *Eight Miles High* by The Byrds, and a rousing version of The Beatle's *Baby You're A Rich Man*. We kept prodding Pete the drummer to flex his muscles a bit and do a drum solo during John Entwhistle's *The Ox*, but he kept flagging just as it got interesting. Then disaster struck. His father turned up early at rehearsal one day and heard our version of *Eight Miles High*, declared it a 'drug song' and forbade his lad from playing with such a bunch of degenerates. This was

MM 17 May 1966 Bob Dylan at the Free Trade Hall

a very serious blow as we'd just got our first gig lined up at a youth club in Whalley Range. After they'd left, Mike and I sat disconsolately in the loft. Suddenly a door in the wall opened and a speedy young bloke, grinning ear to ear came bursting in -

"Hiya. I'm your next door neighbour - Tosh Ryan's the name. You lot are fucking awful."

This is how I first came to meet one of Manchester's legendary figures. Tosh was ten years older than me, a real musician and married with two kids. He'd played sax with the Victor Brox Blues Train, and was currently on a sabbatical. He really did live in the attic that connected through from next door to Miss Patterson's. In the years to come, Tosh became one of the most important people on the Manchester music scene. Behind him stood two other blokes. My first impression of them was that they were totally manic, grinning and chewing and bobbing from foot to foot.

"Don't mind if we come in, do you? This is Jeff and this is Nev. You like Bob Dylan don't you? Fucking wanker. Nev's got tapes of him from off the telly".

Tosh hardly gave us a second to speak, object, or anything. Words and statements flew out of him like a machine gun. "Is that your bass? That's a weird bass. Have you seen what he's done to this Neville?".

I'd stripped the body of my Fender cow-horn bass and painted it in psychedelic patterns, then re-varnished it.

"Do you want a joint, man?" asked Neville thrusting a huge spliff towards us.

I might have wanted to experience an ecstatic vision of Heaven or Hell, but I certainly wasn't going to take drugs! Well, not that drug, anyway. "Erm, no thanks, man ..." (how easily slipped into the hip vernacular) "... We get high on life". God! What a limp, lame statement. The truth of it was, I didn't even smoke cigarettes and always at the back of my mind was somebody's advice about your first smoke - it'll make you throw up - and I didn't want to lose my cool by upchucking in front of these very obviously hip guys.

"Suit yourself, man," he said, passing it over to Jeff.

"Just 'cos you're shite doesn't mean you have to look so fuckin' miserable!" shouted Tosh, "Look at Herman's Hermits!" They all fell about laughing.

"We've just lost our drummer," we told them.

Tosh stopped in his tracks and looked thoughtful for a moment. "I can get you one," he said, "... used to play with John Mayall." We sat bolt upright. "It'll cost you though. Whose is that coat?" Lying next to my amp was a World War One Royal Flying Corps leather overcoat that I'd scored at a jumble sale for about five shillings.

"Mine," I said quietly.

"Give us that coat and I'll give you his phone number."

That evening, coatless and shivering inside a phone booth, I phoned a man called Bruce Mitchell. When he came on the line I told him we were a band, we didn't have a drummer, but we had a gig. Would he like to play with us?

"What's the pay like?" a gruff voice grunted down the line.

"We're getting twenty five quid. We're splitting it three ways," I replied.

"Where is it and what time do you want me there?"

"Don't you think we should have a rehearsal?" I asked him.

"No need for that. Just shout out the tempo before each number - What's the name of the band?"

"Jacko Ogg and The Head People," I told him.

P 1967 Jacko Ogg and the Head People

"Christ!" I heard him mutter down the line.

He turned up - we played and it sounded Okay. Thus began an association that so far has lasted over forty years.

There we were at Art School, junior though it was, exploiting the technical resources available by producing lots of posters in the printing room, when a little later into our first incarnation of 'group' we became able enough to put together a primitive light show. When I use the word 'primitive', I really mean it because we were hindered by the fact that we'd heard about light shows and seen pictures in the *Sunday Times*, but none of us had ever actually seen one, so we had to create a multi-media kinetic art system out of the material to hand. One of Mike Reynolds' friends had taken a bunch of photos of Blackpool illuminations that we had made into slides. At our second, or third gig, another youth club, these were projected over the band while we played. In order to make them a bit more psychedelic as per the *Sunday Times* images, another mate, called Dave Backhouse, turned the lens out of focus and waggled his hand up and down in front of it. For a while it looked quite good, but then he got bored and started making shadow shapes of rabbits and quacking ducks so that really wasn't so good.

We were enjoying ourselves immensely of course, but the fact that the average youth club audience basically wanted nothing other than an endless succession of top twenty retreads they would dance to, meant we had to start looking round for somewhere with a more conducive atmosphere. An audience was sought for the appreciation of drum solos and highly individualistic interpretations of arcane, obscure and demanding material from the cutting edge of contemporary Rock, coupled with our bespoke, mind-blowing vista of throbbing lights.

While we waited for something to turn up, 1967 turned into a time of Love Ins, Legalise Pot Rallies and networking. Living opposite a Victorian house opposite my then girlfriend, Nina, was an eccentric figure called Mike Don, who became a purveyor of underground magazines like *International Times*, before going on to become journalist/editor of at least two Manchester alternative newspapers, *Grass Eye* and *Mole Express*. And in the same house as Mike Don was the Mancunian music giant, Roger Eagle though I didn't know who either of them were at first. An imposing six foot-plus-er, Roger sported a big black quiff and pencil moustache, and at all times of the year wore a bright red cardigan and white Levis. Rather than a fashion statement, I believe it was because it was all he had.

Through Nina's front room window I used to watch with fascination as the man in red ushered in and out of his bedsit a succession of suited-up young men clutching instrument cases. Obviously musicians. One day, in recognising one of them as Milton James, leader of The Milton James Soul Band, I wandered over the road as they were loading their equipment and for the first time fell into conversation with Roger. He explained that he was the Roger Eagle, inventor of the all-nighter and former DJ at Manchester's Twisted Wheel Club. I knew that Eric Clapton used to stop over at his previous flat when he was playing in Manchester and I now learnt that it was to listen to Roger's enviable and prototypical record collection ...

I recalled immediately that I'd seen Roger before, at The Wheel, on one of my couple of visits to the club. I'd watched him sat in his DJ booth spinning a succession of wonderful R'n'B singles like *Help Me Babe*, by Sonny Boy Williamson, *Gettin' Mighty Crowded*, by Betty Everett, and *Road Runner* by Bo Diddley. People still talked about the night the Rolling Stones had come down to bask in their glory and Roger had played, one by one, the original R'n'B versions of all their current set. While Mick Jagger and Keith Richards had stalked out of the place, Brian Jones had come up to Roger and congratulated him on his taste. This was Roger ...

Roger told me that he'd finished DJ-ing there and was now concentrating on managing his 'discovery', Milton James, an American ex-service man who was trying to make it as a Soul singer in England, though I later discovered that the only thing holding Milton back was the fact that he couldn't sing. But anyway, what the mighty Roger did then, the man who had discovered early in his career that you could attract an audience with an all-purpose poster that read simply - 'Tonight! A Beat Group! Admission 2/6d' - he said he'd like to come and see Jacko Ogg and The Head People next time we played ...

The Blue Note on Gore Street was situated like so many clubs at the time, down a flight of stairs, in a fairly large basement, and Jacko Ogg had just set up in residency there, appearing on the Wednesday 'Happenings' nights. We'd celebrated by adding an extra member of the band. Les Brown thought we wanted him for his guitar-playing prowess. He could noodle away for hours on Cream's *Cat Squirrel*, but we wanted him specifically for two other reasons - one, he had a microphone and an amplifier – and second, he was the North of England junior bagpipe champion, and that was the direction I wanted to go in – Rock with pibrocht! However, despite being really good on his chanter, Les steadfastly refused to use it on any number other than the climax of our act, *Baby You're A Rich Man*.

This particular psychedelic ditty was rapidly developing into a monster of a number. Dave Backhouse had finally figured out how to make liquid slides and stood at the back of the room wearing a white lab coat and

Roger Eagle

looking every inch a mad scientist, while he twiddled and tweaked waterfalls of colour around us. Bruce had entered into the spirit of Ogg and for the finale would slip into a gorilla suit complete with mask. Sat behind his kit, thrashing away for all he was worth, it looked quite neat. Mike and I blazed away at the riff, with me singing in a raga-like wail as Les marched up and down skirling away with his bagpipes. Then, when everything looked like it was reaching a crescendo, Mike and I would lean our axes up against our amps resulting in a howling wall of feedback. Dave would rush upstairs in his lab coat and reappear a few seconds later bouncing down the stairs on his Lambretta scooter which he then proceeded to drive round the dance floor, revving up the engine to add to the noise. Bruce meanwhile would quietly slip away from his drum stool and crawl over to the house piano and ignite a series of maroons that exploded with ear crushing intensity. Then, usually, the management would pull the plug at just the right point, and that, ladies and gentlemen, was a Happening, Ogg style.

… And Roger, who did turn up one night, seemed to like it.

A Quick Couple Of Anecdotes From Roger Re Screaming Jay Hawkins

In 1964, after months of trying, Roger managed to book Screaming Jay for a gig at the Wheel. A flurry of telegrams from the American singer's manager flooded Roger's tiny office. In one of the final ones, just prior to Screaming Jay's arrival, his manager subtly pointed out to Roger that the singer would be in need of 'something to smoke', that what Screaming Jay smoked might be hard to come by in England and so they'd be grateful if Roger would make the necessary arrangements. Roger did as he was bid and went to the American Air base at Burtonwood just outside Manchester and bought three two-hundred packs of Camel cigarettes. Screaming Jay's manager was right. Real American cigarettes were hard to get hold of in England at the time. Unfortunately that wasn't exactly what Screaming Jay had in mind.

Another proviso was that Roger had to pick him up personally at Manchester Airport. Again, Roger dutifully did as he was bid and arrived with a taxi to collect the eccentric American on his arrival.

Things were going smoothly until as they drove into Manchester and travelled through Rusholme, Screaming Jay suddenly pulled out a pistol and began firing wildly through the window. Roger and the cab driver were totally shocked and unnerved but, presumably afraid of getting shot, the driver carried on driving and Roger, appalled, asked Screaming Jay what he thought he was doing - "Just keeping them on their toes," he replied nonchalantly, "Just keeping them on their toes."

Roger Meets My Mother

In the winter of 67/68, Roger, dressed in his usual garb, came round to my mother's house to see if I was in. It was snowing and bitterly cold. He knocked on the door. My mother opened it and, never having met Roger before, was rather taken aback at this striking figure. Roger drew himself up to his full, majestic height, and introduced himself –
"I'm Roger Eagle," he said.

"And I'm Big Chief Sitting Bull," replied my mother slamming the door in his face.

P Greasy Bear - CP Lee standing on the shoulders of Ian WIson

Greasy Bear And The Magic Village

When summer came, Les went off to teacher training college, taking his amp, mike and bagpipes with him. Mike King and I got bored with each other and the Head People split up. I hooked up with Ian Wilson, a brilliant singer and guitarist who lived with his family round the corner from me and mine in Didsbury. Ian was a genius boy footballer, who had been signed up by Manchester City, but whose sporting career had been ul timately curtailed when his leg was smashed up in a motorbike accident. He was still on crutches when I sounded him out about forming a duo. The idea I had in mind was close harmonies and a slight return to the Folk thing, but with a definite Country edge. I was glad not to be lugging equipment round any more. Ian said yes, he had nothing else to do while he was recuperating so I used to go round to his mother's house and we'd spend hours just singing and singing. It sounded good. We did Dylan songs (of course), old English ballads, and some Appalachian standards. In between we smoked mountains of dope. You could get an ounce of African Dagga for four quid, or best Afghani for six, in those days. It made the harmonies sweeter and the melodies stronger, at least that's what it felt like.

Roger Eagle also had not been idle. After quickly dumping the Milton James Soul Band he began to enthusiastically pursue the best in contemporary Rock. He had managed to persuade the owners of a failing Beat club called the Jigsaw to let him take control and manage it as an Underground venue. Under its new name of 'the Magic Village', Roger was to establish it as one of the premier gigs in the North West of England and the people of Manchester were able to see the Edgar Broughton Band (regularly), the Pink Floyd, John Mayall and the Bluesbreakers, Jethro Tull, the Third Ear Band, and many more. He became fanatical about Captain Beefheart and the Magic Band, eventually becoming his most regular UK promoter. I believe their affinity was heightened by the fact that they both smoked Kool cigarettes.

And Roger hadn't forgotten me either. He decided that Ian and I needed a name so he christened us 'Greasy Bear', after two songs by Jefferson Airplane, Greasy Heart and Bear Melt. Pretty soon, despite my misgivings, we'd gone electric and called in Bruce to play drums. Ian was on twelve-string Rickenbaker, I just sang harmonies with him, no bass this time. Bruce compensated for that by playing twin bass-drums. Roger put us on as support at the Village and also at concerts he began to promote at a bigger venue, the Houldsworth Hall on Deansgate. There we were support to bigger names like Country Joe and the Fish, the Bonzo Dog Doo Dah Band, Ivor Cutler, Ron Geesin. The list goes on because there were so many live music venues around at the end of the sixties and if you were good, and we were, you could play virtually every night in the North West and beyond.

Gigs ranged from the ludicrously named Huddersfield Builders and Working Men's Progressive Music Night - and we were very popular there for some reason - all the way to the fabled Roundhouse in London where we were on the bill with Sal Valentino's Stoneground. We played with

Canned Heat, Sha Na Na and Procul Harum, Fleetwood Mac (who were complaining that they were still on £10 a week wages when their record Albatross was number one all over the world), and with Eric Burdon in Newcastle the weekend that Jimi Hendrix died - in memory of whom, a quick anecdote -

The Day I Met Jimi Hendrix Wearing My Mother's Dress

Early in 1967 I was idly flipping through the Radio Times and did a double take. On that Tuesday evening's *Simon Dee Show* the special guest slot lined up was the Jimi Hendrix Experience. This was significant for two reasons - One: The show was broadcast live from the BBC studios in Rusholme, Manchester so that was just down the road and - Two: Jimi Hendrix was the nearest thing to God (ie Bob Dylan) on the planet. Mike King and I decided that we had to go down to the studios and try to meet him. And if we were going to do that we had to do it in style and while Manchester hadn't yet developed an 'underground' with boutiques like Granny Takes A Trip, nor was there much indication of the arrival of the 'Summer of Love', we were going to show Jimi that Manchester wasn't full of 'straights'.

Mike and I determined to improvise and we drew our inspiration from our usual source material – the copy of the *Sunday Times* colour supplement LSD issue - and a handful of photographs from the music press of newly emerging groups like the Mothers of Invention, the Pink Floyd and Love. Clearly beads were needed – and already beads were no problem. I'd read about hippies wearing them somewhere and I now had a shoebox full of them. Mike and I nowadays frequented jumble sales around the neighbourhood and had amassed quite a collection of them, along with all sorts of 'beautiful' things, silk scarves, wing collar shirts and even frock coats. I'd also read about kaftans and that was what I knew I needed but equally I was certain I'd never find one anywhere in Manchester. The problem was solved when I spotted my mother bagging up a load of old clothes for a charity shop and when I rummaged through them, one of her old dresses attracted my attention. It was brownish with swirly patterns, worn back to front with a belt it was a worker, along with a jaunty coloured silk scarf tied around my head to complete the ensemble.

And to completely finish off my hippy image I had some sunglasses, though what I had were not exactly sunglasses. I'd smashed the lenses out of an old pair of NHS frames and replaced them with bicycle reflectors bought in the local cycle repair shop. When I wore them everything around me turned bright red and I saw a few dozen multiple images of whatever was in front of me. Standing still they were fine, but the moment I tried to move two things happened simultaneously. The distortion was so great that I lost balance and as I began to fall over a wave of nausea swept over me. They were great! It was just like tripping surely.

Thus adorned, Mike King and I set off in the drizzle to meet the gypsy, attracting the stares of the 'squares' as we blindly stumbled and fumbled our way to Rusholme where the BBC studios were situated inside an old church, previously used by the Mancunian Film Company. We hung around on the opposite side of the road to the stage door for quite a while and it was drizzling with rain, threatening to ruin the two Bob Dylan albums I'd brought with me. By now we were looking fairly bedraggled and must have presented an absurd spectacle to Jimi Hendrix when he eventually walked out of the door of the Studios with Mitch Mitchell and Noel Redding. Jimi stopped in his tracks and shouted across, "Whoa, what is this? A Hippy Invasion?" and he and Redding sniggered. The trio had a quick conflab before Hendrix set across towards us whilst the others wandered off, presumably to the pub down the road, The Welcome.

Mike and I stood tongue-tied, bewildered and phased by Jimi's presence, "Hey man, where are you guys from?" he said. The first thing that struck me was that he was actually smaller than me - and I'm not big. He was like a pocket Jimi. "We really dig you man ..." "... Your Music man" we stuttered simultaneously. Jimi laughed and smiled and pulled out a cigarette. Even though it was raining, he seemed happy to talk and he offered us a cigarette which we declined, "No thanks man, I only smoke joints," I lied. Jimi struck a match and lit his. "What are those?" he asked, "You dig Dylan?"

I blathered on about how we'd seen Dylan at the Free Trade Hall last May and how we had all his records and we were going to start a group and how we loved Jimi's music, and we loved Bob's music, and had he seen Cream, and and and on and on. Jimi laughed and shrugged and said that he'd met Dylan in America recently and that was Dylan was fine after his motorbike accident then suddenly uncomfortable with the rain said, "Hey do you guys want to come to the pub for a drink?" Mike and I stared at one another, this was beyond our comprehensive and nervously we said, "We're under age - they won't let us in." Shrugging, Jimi said, "Well, hey would you like tickets for tonight's show then?"

Unbelievable as it sounds, at 17 both Mike and I had declined Jimi's

Greasy Bear (L-R) Ian Wilson, Bruce Mitchell, CP Lee

drink in the pub. And now we were turning down tickets for the *Simon Dee Show*! The reason? Before I'd gone out my mother had said that 'tea' would be ready about six o'clock and I wasn't to be late. What a good boy I was. Once again, Jimi shrugged and, just as he was setting off to the pub, I thrust the albums and a pen towards him and asked if he'd sign them for me - and he did! Years later, one of them hangs framed on a wall where I live and the other one got lost during the making of a TV show about Rock memorabilia and I guess maybe it's on a wall someplace.

Greasy Bear (L-R) John Gibson Steve Whalley, CP Lee

'Get up Monday morning roll a joint

Don't need to work cos I really don't see the point

The kind of life I'm living's fine by me

Cos I'm a good old fashioned motherfucking hippy'

© 1969 Greasy Bear.

Forward, back to Greasy Bear in 1969 and we were sounding shit hot, very Country style, vocals with four part harmonies ringing out everywhere, and fusion Rock arrangements of American and English Folk tunes, plus a large dollop of original compositions. We added more musicians to Ian, Bruce and myself to get the sound we were after. John Gibson on bass and harmonies and Steve Whalley, on lead guitar and harmonies. But there was one problem - me. I'd 'dropped out', was living in a commune in Salford and had so completely embraced the alternative underground lifestyle that I'd become the people our parents warned us about. My heroes were the Yippies, the White Panthers, the Black Hand Gang and the East-Side Motherfuckers. I believed totally in dope, Rock 'n' Roll and fucking in the streets.

I really believed that we could overwhelm the bourgeoisie with hefty doses of love, a huge dollop of acid and comedy. This manifested itself in the band's set with numbers like *Just Doing My Job* (Like Eichman) which climaxed with me carrying a huge lump of wood, painted brown with the words 'ten bob deal' written on it, and 'rolling' a gigantic joint on stage, and *Three Wheels On My Tank*, a parody of the New Christy Minstrels' *Three Wheels On My Wagon*, geographically shifted to Vietnam. I would wear the gorilla suit (Vietcong guerrilla, geddit?!) and, as usual, the whole thing would end in a wall of feedback and exploding maroons.

RT Greasy Bear (L-R) Ian Wilson, Bruce Mitchell, John Gibson, CP Lee, Steve Whalley

It became obvious when we got a record deal with Philips and went to their studios in London to record an album that the rest of the band had different ideas from me about what material to record. While I was hanging out in Notting Hill Gate with Mick Farren, Steve Mann, Boss Fairy and sundry other British radicals, the band were feverishly excising me from the sessions. When we got back to Manchester they delivered an ultimatum - no more jokes - no more comedy numbers - from now on Greasy Bear was going to be a serious Rock band. And straight off I decided to quit music for good.

By the way, if you want to search out the Greasy Bear album - don't bother. It was shelved by Philips who thought the band was too radical musically for the UK market. They were looking for Heavy Metal and they'd got The Byrds. Tough shit.

Giving Up Playing – Drugs And Politics

In March 1968 the largest anti-Vietnam war rally took place in and around Grosvenor Square - Where was I, you may ask? - Well, I've got two stories to tell about that - one concerns me but first, this one about another Lee on the Manchester scene (no relation).

There's a wonderful piece of archive TV footage that shows this story - Granada TV's *World In Action* follows the adventures of a group of Manchester University Students on the day of the Rally. Led by Student's Union President, Anna Ford, who is shown accompanied on her guitar, singing Bob Dylan songs, the students board their coach and travel off to London to protest about the Vietnam war. The TV people follow their movements around the capital and their return at the end of a long hard day of protesting and street fighting. This other Lee went along with them and when they reached Hammersmith and de-bussed, he got off along with them and they went their merry way. When it came time to meet up again, he showed up with his head wrapped in a bandage and his face smeared with blood ...

After urgent and heartfelt enquiries the story he told then was one of daring-do and death-defying activities to avoid the paw of the pig. But we found out later that in fact he had set off for the demonstration and then fallen down the steps of Hammersmith Tube Station. Taken to Hammersmith General Hospital Casualty Department he was detained for the rest of the day while they x-rayed his head and fitted him with a bandage that happened to make him look suitably like a victim of the demonstration. For reasons best known to himself, he refused to let the nurses wash the blood off his face. When he arrived back at the coach looking like he'd just survived the Battle of Algiers, of course he received a hero's welcome.

My activities that day - I had travelled down to London the day before the demo having been invited by Edgar Broughton to stay at his place in Notting Hill. I arrived wearing an anarchist badge on my black coat over black jeans and with that 18-year-old expression of anti-establishment under my bonnet of long hair ... which fitted the police description of just the kind of mad anarchist they should fear. Sure enough soon after getting off the coach, as I attempted to walk across Horse Guards Parade, I was stopped by the police and held while they checked my credentials. Special Branch finally let me on my way, but I had remained tight-lipped throughout and they could have had very little idea what I was actually there for. The real reason I was in London that time was specifically to be a part of Edgar's group who were going to carry out a magick ceremony designed to bring peace unto the day of the Rally. So when they let me go I made my way on to his flat on Colville Terrace ...

Out! Demons, Out!

Edgar Broughton moved over to his window where I stood transfixed in fascination of a film crew who were retaking a particular shot.

"That's John Lennon's Rolls Royce," he told me.

"What's the film?" I asked.

"Dunno bout that," he replied. "They've been filming at Germaine Greer's house for weeks now."

The film was *Performance*, one of the greatest British films ever made.

Surrounded by this 'magickal citadel' atmosphere, or that's how it seemed to me, there took place much drug-taking and talking and focusing on our activities for the Sunday, the day when Tariq Ali and the Redgraves would be solid with us in the Square, demonstrating against American imperialism in Vietnam. We were, obviously as long-hairs, totally against American involvement and as genuine freaks, not in favour of violent direct action. Our motto was 'Evolution! Not Revolution!' and of course we all believed that social change could be brought about by a change in consciousness aided by LSD and other mind altering drugs. We made our way to a meeting in Belsize Park where we learnt the details of the pilgrimage we would be making the following day.

We were to go at dawn to a magickal place, the Rollright Stones in Warwickshire, and perform a ceremony there that would 'swing' the negative energies away from the violence that was looming in London. And thirteen of us were, at six o'clock am on the day of the Rally, gathered around a pre-Xtian stone circle, making incantations (yeah, alright, basically chanting 'Out demons out!' with Edgar) with a view to stopping a bunch of Left-wing, London and sundry bussed-in trendies from getting their heads kicked in by the police. That done, ceremony completed, we made our way back to London and the Roundhouse where a live TV programme was being broadcast with footage from Grosvenor Square, intercut with us mooching around at the Roundhouse. It was set up like a kind of Speaker's Corner at Hyde Park. Tariq Ali had rushed from the eye of the hurricane to ensure that he appeared on the nation's goggle boxes, and was placed in one corner (not that the Roundhouse actually had any corners, but I'm sure you know what I mean), and was exhorting the crowd of freaks and weirdos to rush out and smash the American Embassy. We plonked ourselves down in a circle at the opposite end and began chanting. No doubt due to Edgar having the foresight to bring along wooden torches that we set on fire, we got the coverage too ... and I believe this was my first appearance on television.

Giving Up Playing – Drugs And Comedy

The absurdity of everything was what my feverish creativity wanted to focus on in performance. So it was essential to feed loads of colourful madness into the mix and connections in London were such that it was easy to get a bottle of pure Sandoz acid for fifty quid. In order to get one hundred whole acid trips in liquid form in one go, our Manchester community would make a quick whip round, mainly made up from people's university grants, add a little more for a return coach ticket and to get the goods.

On one occasion a group of us went down on the mission with a guy called Frank who dosed himself with a couple of thousand microgram drops too many, meaning to make the journey home go better. As he staggered off the coach in Manchester he fell, bashed himself into a lamp-post and the bottle of Sandoz inside his breast pocket totally smashed. Following a few moments of desperatation, a solution was hit upon fast – like a Morrissey shirt thrown to his adoring fans in present times, Frank's jacket got shredded to pieces for all to share. That weekend people scored and ingested little bits of Frank's material - MDMA mixed with his DNA, far out. How we laughed.

And as the comedy in my head got higher, the 'Rock' music scene reached its lowest point ever. There was a pomposity about the new Rock that was emerging, not just in America, but in the UK, that was mind-numbing and soul destroying. What had grown out of sweaty dives and black painted cellars in the early 1960s was now filling arenas with coach loads of lemmings, swallowing the corporate image hook, line and sinker. Rock had grown too fat for its boots and was taking itself far too seriously. What was it about Rock that could be taken seriously? - smash it I thought!

3

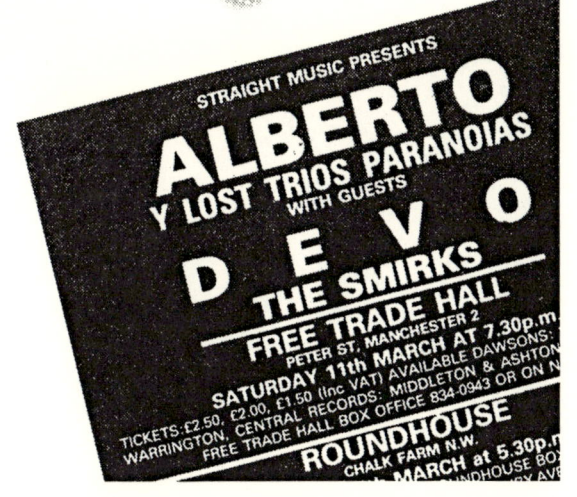

CHAPTER THREE
THE BIRTH OF THE BERTS - Woodstock Uber Alles!

STRAIGHT MUSIC PRESENTS

ALBERTO Y LOST TRIOS PARANOIAS
WITH GUESTS
DEVO
THE SMIRKS

FREE TRADE HALL
PETER ST, MANCHESTER 2
SATURDAY 11th MARCH AT 7.30p.m.
TICKETS: £2.50, £2.00, £1.50 (Inc VAT) AVAILABLE DAWSONS, WARRINGTON, CENTRAL RECORDS; MIDDLETON & ASHTON, FREE TRADE HALL BOX OFFICE 834-0943 OR ON N

ROUNDHOUSE
CHALK FARM N.W.
MARCH at 5.30p.m.

I cannot emphasise enough how strongly the music scene stank through 1969 and 1970. Vital, exciting innovation and sheer love of playing had given way to rambling, egomaniacal noodling. By 1972 I was working in a shop and my creative life was comedy writing backed up by a comedic lifestyle in a squat where we were all maddened by our all-engulfing hatred for the blandness and mediocrity that were the order of the day. Rolling Stone magazine was the arbiter of taste and the nouveau hip scribblings of most of its journalists pumped out copy that was simply adverts for a Californian, tie-dye lifestyle that was about as remote to us in the post-industrial, urban wastelands of Britain as the planet Jupiter. Occasionally writers deviated from the party line, most famously Lester Bangs whose columns I would pin up in our toilet to be re-read at leisure.

Occasionally I'd be coaxed out of my self-imposed 'retirement' and play the odd gig with people like Martin Hannett who'd come round to the squat I was living in. Martin was a member of Music Force, a musician's co-operative, which was started in 1972 by Tosh Ryan, Victor Brox and Bruce Mitchell. Music Force was formed in response to a clarion call from some Trotskyite tendency group but is better described here by Martin Hannett who reminisced about it in 1975 ...

"Supplied with a suitably idealistic constitution, about 80-90 members, a little money from an initial £1 contribution, and a crude sketch of the route to the top we set about the brain-numbing task of promoting a surly, incoherent mass of local talent encompassing a huge spectrum of skills. Any kind of music, equipment hire, transport, poster printing, all these operations were conducted with a kind of guerrilla

GM Tosh Ryan and CP 007

consciousness, and a peculiar nihilism reminiscent of a Japanese suicide squad."

At that time I was working in a 'head' shop selling split-knee loons, cheesecloth shirts and incense. It was a workers' co-operative called On The Eighth Day and as a vegetarian emporium and café it's still going strong. It was whiling away the hours behind the counter there that myself and fellow workers Bob Harding and Jimmy Hibbert found we shared much in common, based in a general dissatisfaction with the contemporary music scene and a strong interest in mind expansion. Bob was another dropout like me, and Jimmy had actually graduated from

1970s Music Force offices, Oxford Road, Manchester

drama school at Manchester University. We were all so pissed off with the moribund state of the recording industry, but encouraged and inspired by a team of freaks from San Francisco called the Firesign Theatre. On their albums such as *Don't Crush That Dwarf! Hand Me The Pliers* and *We're All Bozos On This Bus*, we got into their bizarre, surrealist world of audio madness. A reaction happened and me, Bob and Jimmy started writing and performing comedy scripts with our jokes aimed at the freak community we worked and lived in. We thought we could create an English equivalent of Firesign Theatre and our sketches could be like theirs were - sharp, smart and drenched in acid. Bizarrely, we started getting gigs to perform them at because ...

In keeping with their idealistic constitution, Music Force thought we were a perfect act to be on their books. 'But we aren't musicians!' we said - 'Great!' they replied, and so we found ourselves on the bill of gigs all around the Manchester area and beyond, like when we travelled to Scotland to perform at a gigantic anti-Polaris missile festival. Most importantly came events at the Houldsworth Hall off Deansgate, where Roger Eagle had held a series of concerts before Music Force took over the venue and Roger moved on to Liverpool where he got busy re-energised the city's music scene by staging promotions at a boxing arena known as the Liverpool Stadium, and laid the groundwork for the opening of the world famous Eric's Club later in the 1970s and Roger didn't return to Manchester for some time.

The Houldsworth Hall gigs à la Music Force always had the aura of a 1960s' 'Happening'. Ad hoc ensembles of musicians working under the name, the United Mates of Hysteria would free-form their way through meandering bursts of what is still known as 'Modern Jazz'. More Rock-oriented outfits such as the wonderfully named Shape Of The Rain (bit too much acid there lads?), Greasy Bear (yes, they were still going despite the crushing blow of losing their comic genius) and Victor Brox (then working on a Rock Opera about Hieronymous Bosch, before he went off and joined the Aynsley Dunbar Retaliation) would perform on the main stage, while poet John Cooper Clarke plied his trade around the confines of the hall, along with me, Bob and Jimmy working under the name Hari Odin and The Thunderers. Part of our act was a bizarre game show called 'Beat The Guru', where only 'one spiritual leader can score enough karma to become top dogma!'

Things were going real well and I was enjoying not being a band - we didn't need any equipment for one thing, but the main thing was we were getting loads of gigs, to the point when an A and R man from Chrysalis Records came to Manchester and we were invited to perform a thirty-minute script in front of him in a hotel room. So we did perform, just for one guy, in a hotel room at about two-thirty in the afternoon where and when we failed to create an appealing impression or in any way affect the atmosphere away from what it was towards something like what we were. But audiences carried on liking us and the gigs kept coming our way. We just reckoned that punters were appreciating a break from all those interminable guitar solos. We were just a bunch of freaks who got up on stage and performed a weird story about chickens taking over the world and our audiences found it amusing.

Great Gags From The Albertos' Past

"Waiter! Bring me another stiff brandy - This one's gone all floppy!"

"Quick! They're coming! Slip into these shadows! - Damn! They're too tight!"

"I think I'm losing my mind! – Wait! - There it is, on the chair where I left it!"

We began a residency at a University building called the Squat. The Squat was originally the Royal Northern College of Music, but had been scheduled for demolition to make way for a car-park. Music Force had joined student protestors in their attempts to save the building, and, uniquely, won. The Student Union handed it over to the 'people' for use as a kind of alternative arts centre. It was to play a unique part in the history of Manchester music over the next decade, becoming not just the Berts' Palace of Fun, but a venue for many Punk acts in the late 1970s. Here's Paul Morley in Sounds in 1977 -

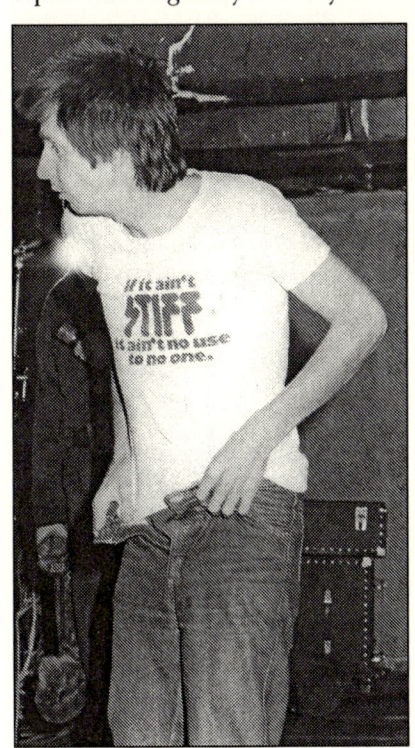

GM Les Prior adjusting himself

"There's a gig tonight at The Squat. Be there! The Squat is an ancient Colditz type building just outside the centre of Manchester. It's an all purpose gig, tonight it's the turn of Warsaw to play their sixth gig and The Worst to play their second. Next week it's a jumble sale! ... Soon Warsaw are on. They have slightly better gear than The Worst and, since they've done a couple more gigs, are a bit tighter. Tony Tabac is on drums ... he only joined a few weeks ago. Peter Hook is on bass/plastic cap, Barney Rubble is on guitar and Ian Curtis is the voice. Lotsa action and jumping in the air to 'Tension', 'The Kill'."

All that was to come. Back in 1972, we were appearing there every Thursday night and having a ball. We even had that name now - Alberto Y Lost Trios Paranoias.

Where Did You Get That Name?

We realised that we couldn't keep changing our name every time we did one of our comedy shows. Like every other band before us and since, we struggled long and hard to come up with a winner. When we'd 'finally' settle on an absolutely perfect one that would be guaranteed to stick in the public's consciousness, we'd throw it away. So we ended up with a ridiculous joke/pun name that had come to me when I was in town and walking past the Free Trade Hall and saw a poster advertising a concert by the South American 'Folk' outfit, Alberto Y Los Trios Paraguayos. These mild, unassuming sons of the Pampas had carved out a little niche for themselves in Europe, appearing quite regularly on TV shows like *Sunday Night At The London Palladium* and *The Val Doonican Show*. Middle England had taken their feisty gaucho looks and trim moustaches to their collective bosom and felt a hitherto unknown surge of Latin blood pump through their veins whenever the group ran through such favourites as *Guantanamera* or *Malaguena*.

"Los Paranoias!" I yelled, laughing at the absurdity of it. Everybody else laughed too that evening when I told them, so we decided to stick with it,

GM (L-R) Bob Harding, CP Lee, John Curd

and the rest, as they say, is history. And in the 1997 Beatles Anthology you can hear John Lennon likewise yell out "Los Paranoias" when him and Paul, George and Ringo were playing the lets-think-of-a-good-group-name game. So, as it says in the bible, great men think alike. Oh, it also says, fools seldom differ.

The funny thing is, nobody from the real group ever protested about our 'appropriation' of their name. Occasionally confusion arose. Early on in our showbiz journey we turned up at a gig and discovered we'd been booked for the Herefordshire Licensed Victuallers Association annual dinner dance.

There they were, table upon table of bucolic men in blazers sat with freshly blue-rinsed wives, eagerly awaiting their soup-in-a-basket and a night of passionate Latin dancing. "Nothing to worry about, lads" the beaming, long-haired promoter assured us. "I've told them you've had a line-up change and do a few blue jokes. It'll be alright", he added. We then realised that he was the son of one of the licensed victuallers who'd blagged his way into being put in charge of the 'entertainment'. The truth of it was, that he wanted to see us and the dinner dance provided him with the perfect opportunity. We did our act as usual. And I do recall a couple of brave souls trying to dance to our side-splitting send-up of every Heavy Metal band ever, *Mandrax Sunset Variations*.

RT The original Lost Trio (L-R) Lee, Hibbert, Harding

On another occasion a coach party of ladies of refined quality were given a refund when they turned up at the Roundhouse expecting a South American evening. The only thing South American present that evening had long gone up our noses, and I recall feeling quite sad as they were led out of the building by a very apologetic promoter, John Curd.

The other thing about our name was how people continually mis-spelled it, or simply couldn't pronounce it. 'Lost' generally became 'Los', and one great night at a club in Darlington the MC came on stage and introduced us with the unforgettable lines -

"Ladies and gentlemen - You've heard them on the radio - You've seen them on the TV - Now, here at the Inn Cognito (you couldn't make that up) you can see them live on stage! It's Alberto and, er... Alberto Why" - he quickly consulted a piece of paper - "And why his lost paratroopers!

It was Tosh who suggested we do a one-off music gig that takes the piss out of the 'Rock' recording/music industry and we talked about it, me, Bob and Jimmy. We had lately been turned on by National Lampoon's album *Lemmings*, a send-up of a Rock festival, with music that consisted of first-rate parodies and scenically where everybody ended up killing themselves. Christopher Guest did Dylan, John Belushi became a devastating Joe Cocker. If we were going to be influenced by anything this was it. We got together an outfit just for a one-off. We stressed to each other we wanted no commitment and we'd do it just for fun. We were happy slumming along at the Squat and gooning about doing odd gigs here and there. We definitely didn't want any more commitment.

Ladies and Gentlemen – Mr Norman Sleak!

Flashback to 1969 - I'm sitting in a corner of an Indian restaurant while the waiter argues fiercely with a hooker. In another corner a drunk dozes fitfully, face down in his dinner. Only it's not an Indian restaurant. It's the attic of a shared student house near the university. I'd gone there after the pub had shut because a student friend had told me I could get a late night curry at his place.

When we arrived we were ushered upstairs by the 'waiter' who also turned out to be the cook as well. Sitar music droned away in the background, several tables were laid out and a menu was proffered. Chicken curry or dhal. I chose the chicken, which years later I'm told comprised of pigeons the cook had trapped in nearby Whitworth Park. Other customers came and went, there was entertainment, it was an 'experience' of the times, and all it cost was just two shillings. I crashed overnight in the living room and the next day the waiter/cook was introduced to me as Les Prior. To this day I don't know if he was a student, or if so, of what. He was definitely the funniest person I ever met, up to and including now.

From then on, Les was just always 'there'; he'd moved into the squat with me in South Manchester, and we were still there at the embryonic stage of the Berts in 1972. Les had continued his themed restaurant meals through the years, and by then they had developed to invitation-only events to which people would arrive dressed appropriately as described on the invitations Les would send out. Transport caff night proved a big success – 'Beans with everything!' trumpeted a chalk board hanging on the wall. Les steadfastly refused to give reduced rates to people who couldn't show their Heavy Goods Vehicle Licence.

Another time and another success (from our point of view) was 'Spirit of the Blitz' night. Nut roast was on the menu, along with corned beef and mash. For invitations, Les and I had sent out ration books, though I still had to dissuade him from demanding to see customers' ID cards at the point of entering the building. "One of them might be a spy," was his reasoning. "Spy or no spy, they're paying punters, Les, just let him in with their ration books," I told him.

During the evening's festivities, while we were relaying a recording of Winston Churchill's 'Blood, sweat and tears' speech through an old 1940s radio set, a couple of unsuspecting freaks came round to make innocent enquiries about cabbalistic magic. Just as they were getting used to the bizarre group of people dotted around the place, Les sounded our air raid alarm. We'd both found old ARP tin-hats in a junk shop which we promptly put on and started ushering people down into the cellar which Les had kitted out with patriotic messages like 'Walls Have Ears Too!' and 'Loose Bowels Cost Lives!' While I encouraged our house guests to join in a merry sing-song-along of *Roll Out The Barrel* and what not, Les convincingly played a BBC special effects album of explosions and jumped up and down on the living room floor. Finally he sounded the all clear and we let everyone out of the cellar. Les had hurled lumps of ceiling plaster all over the place, including onto people's dinner plates, and talked impressively about 'near misses' and 'the Hun was so close you could see his face'. What the two guys made of all this I never found out. Off they went, never to return.

Les could never take things too seriously, and when On The Eighth Day made a transition from Hippy Emporium into a wholefood retailers and restaurant he and Tosh Ryan had a couple of tricks up their collective sleeves. As I had walked out on serious rock fascism in music, I walked out when I saw the outline plans for the restaurant - non-smoking and meatless. The brown rice and aduki beans started rolling in to the tune of health fascism and I rollocked out. But it was at this time that Les started working at On The Eighth Day and he took to it with gusto, always happy, busily putting a little Airfix soldier into each bag of muesli, a little less happy when a mouse in a bag of organic oats bit him. But that came to an end about the time the vegetarian restaurant opened. Following a great fanfare in the local alternative press, the first shift of diners had sat down to their lentil cutlets and bean curd sauce, and as Cat Stevens burbled away in the background, the front door swung open and a huge man in blood stained overalls walked in, bent under the weight of half a side of beef and enquired of the swooning staff, "Where do you want this love?" The wholesale meat deliverer was delivering somebody's order ...

I felt that it more than made up for the faux humiliation of several minutes earlier when I'd been given a stern lecture by one of the staff following my request for some (brown) sugar to put in my tea. He'd delivered a rant about how even unrefined sugar was a killer, so I'd asked if I could have some honey and his look was if I'd asked if I could piss on his smoked tofu. But the send-up of the opening day continued apace. Les who, along with Tosh, had masterminded the first wheeze, delivered the final stage of the prank when on that great opening day the punters witnessed an unsuspecting mechanic wheeling in the cigarette machine that had been ordered.

Knowing Les made everyone feel good, he was always 'up'. Jimmy, Bob and I stayed in more to start properly scriptwriting the Berts' 'one-off' music gig, Les would happily be there, providing meals and ideas, obsessing as usual about economising, and always cooking really well despite often quite unorthodox saving measures. Ever on the look-out for something for free he loved competitions. He entered one in The Sunday Times and it was perfect for Les - readers were invited to come up with money-saving measures - and Les's entry? 'Buy The Observer, it's cheaper'. Well, he didn't have much luck with competitions actually. He thought he'd win the competition with his slogan for Andrews Liver Salts - 'Take Andrews. It'll go through you like a dose of salts!" But he often did get stuff for free. And he liked to get away and stay with other people at weekends. Once, he returned from a weekend in the Pennines carrying a huge bag, and later we heard him banging and clattering in the kitchen really loudly but we'd ignored him, focusing on our script. But we really should have guessed what was happening when he walked in to our writing session twice saying that our 'ideas were buzzing around the squat like flies round a dead sheep'. Les was forever bringing home road kill to cook and what he'd got in his bag on this occasion was a huge dead sheep which as he prepared it for the menu had attracted plenty of flies.

But it was at that time when we were trying to get that 'one-off' together that Les died. Well, to be precise Les died seven years later, but he hadn't been feeling well and his doctor gave him a course of tests and finally he was sent to Christie's Hospital in Manchester where he was diagnosed one afternoon as suffering from Hodgkinson's Disease – cancer of the lymphatic glands.

Les came back from the hospital, white with anxiety and fear. The specialists had given him about a year to live. Me and Bob sat with him in my room totally shell-shocked. We were barely over twenty-one, what did we know about dying? We couldn't speak. Les was shaking. Sometimes his head would jerk around like he was looking for something. I kept rolling joints that we drew in fast like for air, as if we hoped that the dope would make it all go away. Somebody put Love's *Forever Changes* on the record player very quietly.

Eventually, Les spoke.

"Have we got any acid?" he asked.

"About ten hits," I think I replied.

RT Performing 'comedy' (L-R) Lee, Harding, Hibbert

"You take one and give me the rest," he said.

"Steady on Les," I said, "It's a really strong batch of microdot."

"What do you think it's going to do - fucking kill me?"

So we took the sacrament, washing the tiny little pills down with tap water. Dusk had fallen by then and it was growing dark in my purple-painted attic room. Les whimpered and went into a foetal position. As the acid came on he was engulfed by deep, heart rending sobs. I lit incense and tried to pray to what fragments of a God I still had left inside me but quickly I discovered without surprise that there weren't any.

As Les went from apparent catatonia, through to slight movements of his hands, grasping and pulling, grasping and pulling, I saw my job as simply one of finding appropriate music. He'd talk when he was ready.

Together, me and Bob looked through our album collections and pulled out stuff we thought was right. We'd both instinctively grasped what Les was doing and if ever there was a time when LSD was appropriate, this was it. It was going to be a long night.

Relays of housemates brought tea and treats up to the top of the house and took turns sitting with us as Les worked out his death karma. Lit joints danced like fire-flies in the darkness and a stream of sounds enfolded us. We lay on cushions and waited for Les to circumnavigate the globe of his universe. The Goddess Kali stood in front of us and shook her girdle of a thousand skulls while Mexican skeletons danced the Cucaracha and spat in our faces. Christopher Lee and Bela Lugosi sang Kaddish for us while we licked the spittle from our chins. Ancient mummies rose from their tombs a thousand times and laughed at the weeping crew. We travelled along on what was bound to be a long night.

After a couple of hours, Les stirred and changed position. Now he lay flat on his back, arms rigid at his side. He barely moved as one of us moved across the room and put another album on the turntable. We took turns to go and gently touch him, whispering words of love into his ears. Bob Dylan sang of Ophelia and Neptune and then of lamp-posts stood with folded arms. We entered the gates of Eden.

Les sat up and gestured towards a cup - "Tea?" he asked. We made him one and he held the cup shakily to his lips. Bob and I sank back into our cushions.

"Heavy" Les said shakily.

"Yeah, man," we answered.

"No, heavier," he rasped. And realising that he meant music, it had either to be The Grateful Dead, which we were kind of averse to, and he knew it, or he meant, something much more heavier and darker than we wanted to hear.

I tried to imagine what twenty thousand mics was doing to his head. I was surprised that he could talk at all.

"Heavier," he managed again.

Iron Butterfly's *Inna Gadda Da Vida* it was then. If this didn't shift the poor fucker out of his reverie, then nothing would. This acid drenched twenty-minute Plus drum solo was about the most powerful heavy thing you could throw at a tripper in those days. It drilled through your head like a scalpel going through cotton candy dipped in syrup. Bob fitted a pair of headphones onto Les.

"May as well go for broke," he shrugged, and I agreed with him. It'd been nearly five hours now.

All the way through side whatever it was of their finest hour, Les twitched and shrugged, until, as the record ended, he slumped down onto his cushions. Bob and I gazed at him expectantly - "Tea?" he pleaded. We handed him a fresh cup that had been brewed by the Ladies Auxiliary of the Parsonage Road Squat.

Les drank and then finally stirred. He looked around at us.

"Got it sorted now – It's all OK."

We knew again, instinctively what he meant. Les Prior had died that night. He'd forced himself to go through the entire process, aided and assisted by acid. It was the only way.

"Now," he said, "We can get on with living!"

That was it. Les, through straining his brain through the psychedelic mincer, had figured his whole life and death out so that from the dawning of the next day until his eventual demise, he never once complained or used his illness as an excuse for anything.

Well, that is to a certain degree. On one occasion shortly afterwards Les came up to me and said, and I swear, he really said it - "Do you fancy doing over a small local sub-post office?"

"What do you mean, Les? Do over?" I replied.

"Let's rob a post-office. I've checked it out and no-one will get hurt. It's a piece of piss. In Ramsbottom. No guards. We can take it so easy," Les pleaded.

"And, Les, what happens if we get caught?" I asked.

"They're not going to send me to prison," he answered, "I'm dying of cancer!"

There was very little you could do to argue with that, except to point out to Les that the rest of us weren't being afforded the luxury of dying.

"Shit!" He said - "I'd forgotten that!"

Soon in later Berts days, Les discovered to his satisfaction that dying was a very handy pulling line -

"Hi. I'm Les. I'm dying of cancer. You could be the last girl I ever make love to …"

AB 1974 Waiting for the revolution

Generally, his illness never became public knowledge, though he occasionally referred to it obliquely. Once at London's Nashville rooms after he'd been away for a while having treatment, one of the crowd shouted out - "Hey Les! Where've you been, man?"

"I've not been well," he shouted back, "I disagreed with something that's eating me!"

So, Alright – Why Norman Sleak Then?

In the best Hollywood musical style of, 'Hey kids! Let's put on a show!" the Berts' one-off Rock gig began to take shape. Because we all loved or hated whole genres of Popular music Bob, Jimmy and I decided the show would just have to cover the entire history of Rock from its beginnings in the mid 1950s, to the present day (1972/73). By doing it that way we could send-up everything from Rock 'n' Roll, to Psychedelia, taking in Country and Western and Pomp Rock. Then we had a brain wave. Why not centre it around one character? Make him a would-be Rock star who tries to 'make it' but never does, no matter what style he chooses!

A character was taking shape, well more a caricature of a certain kind of person that would be well known to virtually everybody at that time - the Mandy freak , the form of which would be identifiable in American culture as 'a downer freak'. In Britain the downer drug of choice was Mandrax sleeping pills. Drop a couple of them and then head on off to the pub for a few pints before setting off to a gig to preferably watch a Heavy Metal band – and if you didn't set fire to yourself first, or fall under a bus, or, possibly, go to sleep, or all three simultaneously, you'd likely as not be vomiting. Mandy freaks did a lot of vomiting. Not necessarily over themselves. These slurring, shambolic wretches, usually male, stumbled and crashed their way through life often sporting heavily-stained RAF great-coats dyed black. They were the shock troops of Rock, the illegitimate spawn of the Goddess Barbitura. The idiot bastard sons of the counter-cultural revolution of 1967. They were failures.

We called our idiot bastard son Norman - Norman Sleak. He was so archetypical that we could all play him to perfection and from then on, Norman was the main character of our Rock 'n' Roll script. Tosh liked to say that there was a little bit of Alberto in all of us, but I think there was more of Norman, so easy was it to slip into his RAF great-coat and spout gibberish. He went on to be the hit of our 1977 stage show *Sleak – The Snuff Rock Musical*. And, if things had gone any better, Norman would no doubt have accepted the Nobel peace prize on our behalf in 1998. When the Berts got a record contract, by mutual agreement because we believed we were a group of syndicalist anarchists, we agreed that all our song-writing credits appear under the combined name of 'N. Sleak' and that we all receive equal shares of the royalties.

With our concept and principal character in place we set about writing the songs. One of our favourite books was a hard-core porn novel entitled *On My Throbbing Engine* by the uniquely named Salambo Forrest. As a tribute we penned a dirty, twelve-bar rocker called, *I'm Gonna Grease Up My Crankshaft*. Bob contributed what was eventually to turn out as one of the Berts' greatest songs, *Jesus Wept*, a Southern Baptist style sing-along that owed more to Satan than to the Lord.

"Now that I've found Jesus, I won't smoke dope no more.
(I won't smoke it no less neither!)
I'm through with smack and fucking
Now that Jesus is my Lord
I'm a Jesus loving boy"

And Les came up with the ditty, *Pavlov's Dog*, that opens with the immortal line - "Every time I smell pussy I go weak at the knees!"

We were about a week away from the gig when we realised that in order to perform this stuff we needed a backing band and I remember thinking, "Here we go again" ...

Just around the corner in another squat was a bunch of guys who were busy hammering away night and day in order to sound like the Allman Brothers and we went and roped in the guitar player called Chris and a bass player called Dave. They were well up for the gig and straight away you could see Chris and Dave as 'serious' musicians shared the ridiculous notion of 'making it' and so we dispelled that notion by reassuring them - and ourselves - again - that it was to be a strictly 'one-off'. The one thing Alberto Y Lost Trios Paranoias were determined never to be, was serious.

For drums, I obviously phoned Bruce. I knew Greasy Bear weren't getting that many gigs any more - especially now they'd lost that cutting edge of comedy(!). And this time, when he said he'd play, I didn't bother inviting him to a rehearsal - I'd just shout the changes.

Tosh turned up at one of the sessions. "What you need is a brass section," he said, and returned ten minutes later with his sax. The next time he came he brought Jeff Walters. With the four of us, the brass section, percussion and guitarists, we'd suddenly grown into a nine piece. I could see this spiralling out of control - and I was right. Martin Hannett had now got involved and the gig had become a 'benefit' for Music Force.

Martin added three female back-up singers: Susannah, his girlfriend, Pat, who eventually became Jimmy's girlfriend, and Fran, who became mine. We christened them 'The Lillettes'. Now we were a twelve piece. Thankfully, the night of the gig arrived and we couldn't grow any bigger or there wouldn't have been room on stage for us all.

And we did that gig - a non-stop revue type of thang, lots of gags and visuals, each of us taking turns to have the lead microphone, and of course the ubiquitous Les diving in whenever he felt like it so he could create havoc with us and the audience. In true traditional Bruce style, there was even a maroon explosion at the climax of the set. The audience went crazy and then it was over.

We sat sweating in the dressing room holding a post-mortem ... I knew what was coming, and it was inevitable really ...

"That was really fucking great! – We should do it again!"

So we did - and the 'one-off' performance became like a blueprint for all the Berts gigs that followed - for the next ten years.

50 WHEN WE WERE THIN

RT

From one trio to a bigger trio

ALBERTO Y LOST TRIOS PARANOIAS

AB

4

CHAPTER FOUR
HALF MAN HALF VAN - THE ROCKY ROAD TO?

STRAIGHT MUSIC PRESENTS

ALBERTO Y LOST TRIOS PARANOIAS
WITH GUESTS
D E V O
THE SMIRKS

FREE TRADE HALL
PETER ST, MANCHESTER 2
SATURDAY 11th MARCH AT 7.30p.m
TICKETS: £2.50, £2.00, £1.50 (inc VAT) AVAILABLE DAWSONS:
WARRINGTON, CENTRAL RECORDS: MIDDLETON & ASHTON
FREE TRADE HALL BOX OFFICE 834-0943 OR ON N

ROUNDHOUSE
CHALK FARM N.W.
MARCH at 5.30p.m

Some of the band actually had jobs, some were on the dole. I was always reminding myself how I didn't want to get back into performing music, but like an out of control juggernaut, the Berts had begun an inexorable sweep forwards in their mission to save Rock. Well, if not save it, at least to take the piss out of it by presenting a real alternative to the monumental lorry-load of crap that was 'Rock'. None of us thought we were doing it forever, it was just fun and if it got us a few drinks and stuff to eat, so much the better. We were, what is known in the biz as semi-pro and we were 'schlepping' around the country, meaning we were on the road and travelling, in our case, up to 2,000 miles a week. Sorry, I don't know the metric for that, even though I should because we ended up schlepping our way around Europe for what feels like a thousand years. In the beginning though, it was mainly around the North of England …

Central to our performance development was always The Squat, which was basically the Albertos' musical laboratory, and apart from the mainstay of playing local colleges and universities, we would play to regular appeal in places that became a kind of home from the Squat home. There was the Seven Stars Pub in Heywood and the Seven Stars in Culcheth, both brilliant local gigs where we would receive a welcome more befitting artists of the stature of, well, anybody bigger than us actually, though we weren't arguing. We picked up massive support at a host of venues not called the Seven Stars, in places like Ashton and Oldham. Another one where we received tremendous support, also not called the Seven Stars, was the Swan in Sheffield but the last time we played there was when the landlord did a runner with one of the barmaids, carrying off with him the takings from the night – all of about £1200 (I'm sure it was the erotic aroma of the gig that sent him on his path to perdition with such a low heist figure, but good luck to him anyway) but a curse upon him, because no part of the takings ever got to the Berts for that gig …

GM It's a long road that has no … CP Lee

Every time we played away from the Squat we had to rationalise our structure – there'd be or more often there couldn't be the Lillettes and/or horns – and with several roadies needed it was always a ridiculously large organisation to be schlepping about. Of course it was beyond the scope of the mission to make money out of gigging - that would be ludicrous - but we did seek a resolution to the size of the group for practical measures ...

Witness now the incredible psychic powers of the Berts clearly demonstrated as, way before Punk would make a musically-talentless front performer a moral tenet of its faith, and well over a decade before the Happy Mondays would be happy to have Bez lolloping around on stage, we had Les, the man who couldn't play an instrument and couldn't sing to save what was left of his life. Les was untouchable, a permanent feature of the group, central to the Berts. And eventually we did drop both the Lillettes and the horns.

Another line-up change came about when Bruce announced his imminent move back to Greasy Bear and a replacement came along in the shape of 'Mongo', aka Ray. I don't know where he came from, but his refusal to speak in anything but Welsh, or very simplified English delivered in a sing-song, high pitched whine baffled everyone. Mongo's presence was both menacing and hilarious, often at the same time. He used to

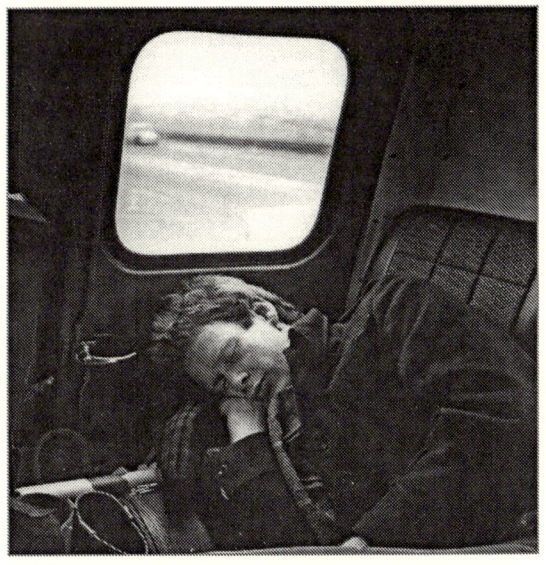

GM Come on down to the big sleep - Tony Bowers

be pulled on stage by a long piece of rope that was tied around his neck. His manic bearded face was topped off with a tea cosy and he'd be naked to the waist down. His lower regions were modestly covered by a pair of pyjama bottoms though a cushion was shoved down the front of his pants to create a frighteningly large cod-piece. The fact that he often sported this ensemble when not on stage was quite disturbing and no-one knew quite what to make of him.

Allow Me To Introduce Mr Nimrod Tush

Ray/Mongo possessed, or was possessed by a third persona - Nimrod Tush. Nimrod would talk in a very precise manner slightly reminiscent of WC Fields. When the mood took him he would dress up in his oilskins and listen to his favourite album *Songs of the Humpback Whale*. So enamoured of the album was he that he liked to share it with unsuspecting guests by playing it at full volume through hidden speakers in his bathroom.

By utilising his secret powers Nimrod could also defuse potentially ugly situations - After playing a gig at Sheffield Poly Dimitri left his jacket behind. About a year later we returned to play the same venue and there was one of the Poly's stage crew wearing the jacket. Cue an outraged Dimitri arguing more and more loudly with the guy about whose jacket it was - "That's my jacket!" - "No it isn't, it's mine!"

Ray/Mongo/Nimrod Tush with his favourite album

Suddenly an oilskin-clad figure stepped in between the warring factions. First he looked at Dimitri, then turned and looked the student helper up and down before announcing in an imperious manner -"Excuse me. I seem to recognize those trousers!"

This, of course, was as nothing compared to the havoc Mongo could unleash on stage when the mood took him. Bored, tired or simply at a loose end, he would suddenly drop his pyjama trousers and cupping his wedding tackle in with one hand stretch them out as far as they'd go with his other and shout, "Last chicken in the shop!"

Mongo's demeanour was of pure appeal to Bruce straight away and Bruce even agreed to stay with the Berts for a few more gigs to 'break him in'. However, after a couple of gigs with two drummers we noticed that 'breaking in' entailed Mongo thrashing away at his drumming on his kit while Bruce would occasionally tap his hi-hat, or perhaps help bring a number to a crashing conclusion. The rest of the time Bruce would be sat back reading a magazine or smoking a spliff, waiting for his drum solo to be introduced - "Here he is boys and girls! The man you've all been waiting for! The man we call Mister Rhythm, because that's what he's done all night - Missed the fucking rhythm!" at which time Bruce would suddenly spring into action. And gradually through the mist of pleasure that was the Berts' performers' lot, it began to eventually dawn on us that Bruce hadn't actually left and gone back to Greasy Bear. He may have done one gig with them, but if that was leaving he was back with us the next night. Still nothing was said about this and the line up and behaviours with our two drummers remained unchallenged - what was one extra musician to us, we were the Berts - and the Berts had no truck with business acumen ...

Selling Our Souls To Satan

Down in London there were people feeling the same way about Rock-shite and a new genre of music called 'Pub Rock' was emerging, championed by outfits like Doctor Feelgood and Chilli Willie and The Red Hot Peppers. Yes, there were a few of us around the country who maybe didn't know exactly what was going on, but we knew as sure as shit, we didn't like the smell of it! So it got talked about - we should schlep around the whole

GM Les in the arms of Morpheus (Bob behind)

country. Even with no money, no food, no sleep in prospect, it seemed like a great idea! Those of us with jobs would give them up and those on the dole would be economical with the truth. Les thought it was a great idea. His life was as precarious as possible anyway. He figured that at least he'd get to see more of the country this way, and he was, I guess, right.

First off, we needed a roady with a van and a PA. Enter one Dimitri Grilliopolis, a Welsh/Greek wonder boy from the APE ('All People Everywhere') commune down the road. He'd been in a massive outfit too, 'Drive In Rock, who were a precursor to Showaddy Waddy, only light years better. I think they'd even appeared on the television talent show Opportunity Knocks, and Dimitri said they would have won too if they hadn't dropped acid before recording the programme. Anyway, Dimitri had a PA, microphones, mixer desk, the lot, and, and - the very big kind of and - he also had a van. Though to be more accurate, it was a very old ambulance and it looked like it had been pensioned off just after the Second World War. Still, we weren't complaining.

Having Dimitri on board meant that we could now travel to gigs in true gigging-style, even if it meant being crammed into the back of a windowless metal box along with a PA, amps, guitars, two drum kits and about five or six Berts - because no more than three people could possibly fit in the front. No matter how carefully we built a nest out of boxes, cushions, sleeping bags and paperbacks, whenever it turned a corner the whole interior would slide round forcing our bodies into another grotesque posture to avoid being crushed to death. I can't tell you what fun it was.

GM CP rocking for the lord

Honestly, I can't. During the winter of 73/74, it was cold. So cold, in fact, that in the back of the ambulance the condensation from our breath froze in icicles on the roof and down the sides, and when we arrived at one gig we had to be chipped out of the back because the door had frozen up. Laugh? I feared we'd never start. One time the headlights failed as we were crossing the Pennines over the Snake Pass in the dead of night. We took it in turns to stand on the running board shining a torch so the driver could see where the hell we were in relation to the sheer drop just at the side of the road.

GM Jimmy deals with a heckler

Then we thought - Why not have more roadies? And another guitarist? Actually, the thought never occurred to us, it just happened by chance. Like I said, we were never renowned for our business sense. Amongst the audience that regularly turned up for our gigs at Culcheth were two brothers, Tony and John Bowers, and a friend of theirs, Simon White. Tony and Simon were outstanding lead guitar players in a Rock band called 'Pachuco'. We invited Simon to play lead guitar and put Chris Wainwright on rhythm. So Tony didn't feel left out we invited him to roady with us if he wanted. He wanted, but it soon became apparent that he could play as well as, if not better, than most people we'd heard, let alone knew, so we did the logical thing. At a certain point in the show, Simon would pretend to fall over and his playing had to be taken over by ... that's right! A roady. Only for one number mind, we didn't want him getting ideas above his station.

Okay - So now we had the requisite gear and the means of getting to gigs what we needed was a way of getting more gigs. We'd pretty well exhausted all the venues that Music Force could offer, so we needed to break out of the North West. It was a truism then, and, despite the best efforts of Punk, it's probably still a truism now, that in order to get well known you 'had to go to London', or, at the very least, get a London agent. And in order to get an agent to see you, you needed a gig in London, but you couldn't get one of those unless an agent had seen you. Obviously it's the Rock *Catch 22*. So we looked for another way. We could take a demo tape to London and do the rounds of agents, hoping they'd let you into their office for long enough to impress them. We didn't have a tape, but we did have Les.

I was temporarily located in London at that time anyway, so Les and Bob journeyed down and we met up to plan our assault on the great and the good of the Capital's Rock scene. A quick scan through papers like NME and Melody Maker resulted in a list of 'essential' agencies. The plan was that Bob and I would make the appointment, turn up and lay our spiel on them. This included handing them our latest poster - 'The Albertos, Designed With Your Mind In Mind' - and raving about how good we were. When they'd listened to enough of this they'd be bound to say, "Have you got a tape we could listen to?" and we'd shout, "No! But we've got our music box!" Les would be waiting outside in a large cardboard box labelled, 'Music - Handle With Care'. We'd drag in the box and from its inside Les would 'do' a couple of our numbers. We were convinced that we couldn't fail. Who wouldn't be impressed by this wacky stunt? We knew that back in Manchester a pathetic bunch of hungry musicians were waiting for the good news. We started ringing around.

Having walked our fingers to the bone, we established that the only people who said they'd see us were called Blackhill Enterprises. They had an office in Bayswater and we went round. I knew a little bit about Blackhill.

P... came third in the Bob Dylan lookalike competition

They'd managed my old mates the Edgar Broughton Band, and had something of a reputation within Hippy alternative circles. Managers of the original Syd Barrett, Pink Floyd, and instigators of the Hyde Park Free Concerts, they seemed like good people to see. When it came to it, Bob and I persuaded Les to leave his box back at the flat and we planned just to go in all guns blazing and not leave until we'd got a gig. We were all fired up and full of piss 'n' vinegar when we got in there and entered the front office.

Very quickly our upfront, Mancunian aggressiveness was dissipated by the languid atmosphere inside, where a beautiful, long-haired woman wearing a headband and a flowing white dress was on the phone. Several men with equally long hair were lying around on bean bags. Around the walls were posters for various events going all the way back to the Ally Pally Technicolour Dream in 1967.

GM Modelling the Autumn range - Men from CIA

"Hi guys - Just take a seat. I won't be a while," she cooed. We sat.

"Yeah, but Kevin Ayers gets top billing or it's just going to mess around with the vibes," she spoke into the phone. I could see that Les was getting fidgety.

"We haven't got all day!" Les suddenly barked. Everyone looked up from their navels at him. "We've got an appointment somewhere else in half an hour," he lied.

"It's cool if you want to go," said the groovy chick, "But I'm sure Peter will only be a minute."

"We'll stay. We'll stay!" Bob and I burbled, pushing Les back down into his bean bag. "Fucking hippies," he muttered under his breath.

AB 1974 CP takes off for Central London

A bespectacled, vaguely academic looking man emerged from a back room. "Hi. Are you the Albertos?" he asked peering at us through bifocals. "Come on through to the garden."

And so we entered the hallowed portals of Blackhill. There was an unmistakable whiff of dope in the back as we made our way through to a tiny London garden.

The man was Peter Jenner. The other half of the Blackhill partnership was Andrew King, but we weren't to meet him that day. Peter listened to our spiel then told us that Blackhill weren't an agency anymore, that now they were strictly managers, but that he'd see what he could do about getting us a gig in London as he was really interested in seeing us. He said he liked what we had to say.

Waging War Against The Mellow Peril

In the pub afterwards we decided, seeing as how we hadn't been able to make contact with anybody else in the Rock business, we'd definitely give Blackhill a chance and pretty soon a phone call was received at Berts' HQ in Manchester.

A gig, courtesy of Blackhill, was forthcoming in London. As it turned out, it was not just any old gig either, what we got was a support slot at the legendary Marquee Club. Now the Berts' home-made publicity machine could swing into action. We'd invite all the music business people we could think of - journalists, agents, managers, record company A and R men (for there were no female ones at that time) - this would be our big chance!

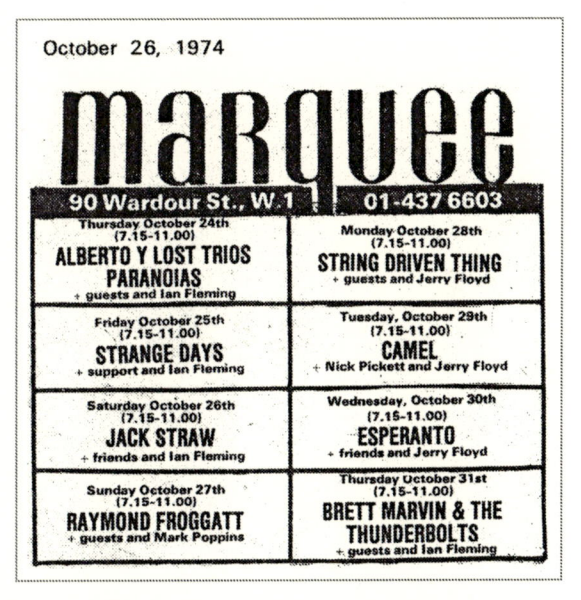

This would be our opportunity to show the jaded hacks of London that a fresh alternative to the humdrum, boring psychopomp of contemporary Rock existed beyond the confines of their little concrete towers. There were however, a couple of drawbacks. Firstly, as an unknown quantity, the short-sighted booker at the Marquee had chosen to give us a support slot to a bunch of French pseudo Art-Rockers called Ange. One had heard of them, of course. There were dozens of this sort of creature slinking round the Rock world, oozing their synthesiser bleatings at comatose buffoons who thought it was 'cool' to be drowsy. Norman Sleak would have loved them. Secondly, as support act we were to receive the princely sum of £5. In 1974 that was the standard fee the Marquee paid for a support. It would remain that way until the Musicians Union had a go at them in the late 1970s and forced them to sharpen up their act and pay basic union scale. However, this was still 1974 and we had to bring an ambulance of freaks and their equipment all the way from Manchester (and back) for five quid. Whatever! We thought it was a bargain. We were going to play at the Marquee! It was a premier showcase venue. Those of us who were working put in the rest of the petrol money ...

... We arrived more than two hours early and had to hang around Wardour Street waiting for someone to come in and open the club. Too poor to buy a drink in any of the local pubs we played dodging traffic wardens with the van until we could unload our gear and get set up. Walking inside was like drinking the past. Like all clubs it was basically a long black hole with a stage, but what a stage. It was here that many of my heroes of the last ten years had played. We sat in the dressing room behind the stage and read the graffiti on the wall, and added a new one alongside the boring and passé 'Eric Clapton is God' - 'Bert Weedon Is God!' Even in this new millennium people talk about that piece of graffiti! So now you know!

Fidgety staff told us that we'd have to leave the dressing room as it was specifically reserved for the headline act and it simply wasn't big enough

GM (L-R) Doug Marnoch, Andrew King, Simon White, Darth Vader, ?, Tony Bowers

for two bands. We weren't going to argue at this point as life was just too damn exciting and it was more fun anyway to go into the club and head for the bar and try and chisel a drink out of Peter Jenner, or any of the other showbiz types we'd invited. But when we stepped out into the rapidly filling club, there was only Pete Jenner - none of the other bastards had bothered to turn up. Hey! It was early. Plenty of time. Peter bought us drinks anyway and was introduced to Mongo. Peter looked suitably impressed by his cod-piece, though politely said nothing.

We were supposed to be on at eight-thirty, and it was nearly eight now and there was no sign of Ange, or even of their equipment. Somebody from the Marquee came up and spoke quietly to Peter Jenner and Peter's face beamed as he announced to us -

"Ange have been held up at Folkestone by Customs and can't get here in time. They want you to headline the gig. You'll go on at nine-thirty."

It was as simple as that. From support to top of the bill in just a few short minutes. We couldn't believe it. What would the audience think? They'd paid to see some bunch of French Art Rockers and they were going to get an unknown band from Manchester. Fait accompli! N'est pas!

"And a crate of beer in the dressing room please," we heard Peter tell them. We were getting to like him even more.

> ERIC IDLE and George Harrison seen enjoying themselves at Neil Innes' Fatso gig at the Nashville Rooms last week.
> At same venue on Saturday, Alberto Y Lost Trios Paranoias proved there is, indeed, a future for parody and satire in rock.
> The doors were closed before 9 p.m. Many were turned away.
> Inside it was a shoulder to shoulder vibe, with oxygen in desperately short supply.
> Alberto were in brilliant form, and really deserve to be recognised as one of the best live bands in the country.

It came to the time and we went on and did our set. At first the reaction seemed muted and then it wasn't and the crowd began to warm to us with our gruff Northern ways. They laughed at all the right places and some of the wrong ones. The Berts had acquitted themselves with honour and we eventually left the stage after an encore at around eleven.

Peter rushed into the dressing room.

"That was really good. I think we'd definitely be interested in you. Anyway, you chaps get changed and I'll see you in the bar. There's a couple of people there who wants to meet you."

One of the guys in the bar turned out to be a slight young man going by the name of Allan Jones. He was a journalist for *Melody Maker*. He spoke to Les first.

"Would you like a cigarette?" he innocently enquired.

"No thanks, man," answered Les. "I'm dying of cancer."

This was Les' stock response and usually doubled us up with laughter. Allan, however, looked slightly taken aback, but he took it in his stride. He interviewed us each in turn that night and a week later we got our first review in a national music paper.

The other person we met for the first time was a man slightly older than us, with a curly mop of hair and a Norfolk jacket. He had the most wonderful accent and called everybody 'old boy' and 'dear chap'. This was our first introduction to the human being called Andrew King - the son of the preacher man, and other half of Blackhill Enterprises.

"I'd Like To Do A Song By Bob Dylan Called 'The Ballad Of Hollis Brown' - No I Won't, I'll Do One About Wanking Instead!"

And so it was, one month later with a management contract signed and a small cash advance supposedly for new equipment senselessly thrown away on luxury items like food, we found ourselves playing in front of thirty thousand people at a Hyde Park free concert, on the same bill as Roger McGuinn and Toots and The Maytals. We made the front page of Melody Maker, and with an ego boost like that, those of us with jobs jacked them in and with nary a thought for health and happiness we set off to conquer the world as a fully fledged 'professional' band.

And what a world it was. Analogous to the sporting world, we were of course strictly at the bottom of the third division. And we were performing in that league where the ethos was 'to work your way to the top', even though we had absolutely no sense of 'making it big' or and we never thought in terms of 'having a hit'. We just wanted to show people how stupid the whole Rock thing had become, and if we could earn a living

---

Albertos' favour to Splodge

ALBERTO Y Lost Trios Paranoias, having used up their old posters on their last gig series, now announce their "Let's Give Splodgeness More Material To Rip Off Tour." The first half-dozen dates to be confirmed are at Egham Royal Holloway College (tomorrow, Friday), Durham St. Cuthbert's College (Saturday), Reading University (June 23), Manchester Lamplight Club (24), Leeds University (25) and London Regents Park Bedford College (26).

from it, so much the better. Call us naïve, call us idealistic, even call us stupid ...

Third division gigs took place in pubs, clubs and civic halls and though exceptionally we became regular headliners at the Marquee, which kept us motivated, all those other venues that we slogged our way to during 1974 veered from the ludicrous to the insane. Some of them were great, however, and the reception we got at pretty well most of them encouraged us to keep on with 'the mission'. We established residencies at a bunch of them like JB's Club in Dudley, heart of what the Berts called 'The Sabbath Belt', owing to the audience's predilection for Heavy Metal, and later to become famous for a Sex Pistols bootleg that was recorded there. The kids at these gigs, like at the Cherry Tree in Nuneaton, JB's, The Outlook in Doncaster, were out for a night that took them away from the boredom of their situation. They knew what they were laughing at when the Berts became 'Norman Sleak and His Stumbling Idiots' and blazed their way through *Mandrax Sunset Variations*, or Perry Como's *Walking In A Winter Wonderland* as performed by 'Captain Beefcake and His Tragic Band'. The Berts provided the perfect backdrop to a night of stoned oblivion and merrymaking.

Albertos spare Scots shock

ALBERTO Y LOST TRIOS PARANOIAS return to the road with a "Hard Luck Scotland" tour.
To make up for Scotland's embarrassing start in the World Cup, the Albertos have, by manner of compensation, agreed to play only dates south of the border for this new tour.
Full dates are: Birmingham Town Hall June 14, Nottingham Playhouse 15, Hereford College of Education 16, Middlesbrough Town Hall 18, Stockport Davenport Theatre 19, Liverpool Empire Theatre 20, Basildon Towngate Theatre 21, Coventry Tiffanys 22, Hull University 23, Newcastle University 24, Stafford Top of the World 26, Bristol Locarno 27, Guildford Civic Hall 30.
John Dowie, ex-Big Girl's Blouse, will be supporting.

THE ALBERTOS

The Winning Post, Twickenham, Tiffanys, Coventry, Tolworth Recreation Centre, Ruffles Club, Aberdeen, all of them met with the Berts and the Berts lived to tell the tale. We only got bottled off once and that was at a gig near to home. It was at the Institute of Technology in Bolton and we found there that the Sabbath belt was just this once quite unbreakable ... how it spawned Buzzcocks a couple of years later I'll never understand! Les thought it was hilarious. We left the stage that night in a shower of broken glass and abuse and he was up there alone, talking into his shoe (something about 'soul music') when a heckler screamed at him to "Get on with it!". Les answered with, "I'm sorry if I'm boring you, but somebody's got to be the new Roy Harper". A near miss from a pint pot effectively coaxed Les from off the stage.

In December 1974, Allan Jones wrote a two-page article for the Melody Maker in which he outlined the iniquities of life on the road. He interviewed us along with Jake Rivera, manager of Chilli Willie and The Red Hot Peppers.

"Whilst the likes of Rod Stewart and The Faces have been cruising around the country on a diet of Bacardi and Jack Daniels, Alberto Y Lost Trios Paranoias have been lurching from Salford to Southampton on a diet of cold tea and very little sympathy.

"They've just completed sixteen gigs in just over two weeks, and travelled countless miles all over the country. They calculate that for most of the gigs they play they spend ten to fifteen hours, often more, travelling, sometimes with no money or food. The total amount of their earnings for those sixteen gigs, after expenses incurred on the various journeys, is reckoned to be in the region of "a cool twelve pounds each".

"It might not be much," said Mongo, one of the Alberto's Drum Giants, "but at least it's regular."

One of Les' dodges for saving us money was to arrange for the ambulance to run out of petrol on the motorway. He'd discovered that the rescue vehicle that arrived to fill you up charged less than the service station forecourts. He used to sell us sandwiches too when he had enough money to buy the stuff for making them.

Despite the starvation and elation, the Berts battled on, and behind the scenes Blackhill supremos, Andrew and Peter worked on their cunning masterplan to bring the band up in the world.

Things Take A Turn For The Berts

When Sir Russell Blatcher reminisced about the battle of the Somme, and wrote, "My dear, the smoke, the noise, and the people!" he could have been writing about the bands we were on the bill with, nay, very often supporting. We used to joke that it was a man's life in a modern Beat group. That you joined a band to travel the world, get stoned and meet interesting folk, but honestly, with a few exceptions most of the people we met only justified our determination to get on with it. Our 'brothers in arms' consisted of such legendary Rock giants as Hobo, Boris (Boris?), Dead Ringer, Equinox, Goliath, Sparrow, Zzebra(!), Seventh Wave, Esperanto (gimme a break!), Thirty Years War (and it felt like it!)

and Sassafras, to name but dozens of dead horse floggers who were about to be obliterated by the coming of Punk. Doubtless there are still some out there who pray for a CD box-set retrospective of Goliath to be re-issued complete with out-takes and a full colour booklet, but really they were shit then and they'd still be shit now.

It was our job to carry some kind of torch for meaning in Rock, and to illuminate the farce of the on-going, up-chucking stadium Rock phenomenon. To focus on the ridiculous grandeur of its performers, the beer moths of Rock such as Rick Wakeman - an easy target especially with him being so large. Who'd believe that Emerson Lake & Palmer would need three separate articulated lorries just to carry their egos in - and we were actually touring with groups who wanted to be like them! Or they all wanted to be American like the Eagles or like Jackson Brown - not anyone decent - they didn't want to be like good Americans like Little Feat, they wanted to be like these jerky, soppy gnats-pissy people. And there were we, the Berts, carrying some kind of torch for meaning in Rock.

One of our earlier guerrilla art projects had been the 'artist as a bag of sugar' concept. We'd been equally disgusted and amused by the Rock World's use of the term 'product' in favour of other, more poetic descriptions, such as, the fruit of an artist's endeavours. The word 'product' reveals the industry's refusal to view the performer as human. It reduces a creative artist into marketing terms and they'd talk about 'how many units' a 'product' had shifted. It was a loathsome and degrading terminology that more than signified their contempt for music and their love of accountancy and it was all anathema to the Berts. Yet we were now hooked in ... and, as 1975 dawned, we were searching for a record contract obviously because, well ...

A record contract is supposed to give a band a more secure financial footing. If you go on a tour to promote an album the record company are supposed to underwrite the costs, help with the publicity, get radio interviews, air-play and so on. It's a mutually beneficial arrangement. Andrew and Peter decided that we needed to make a demo tape for playing to labels who expressed an interest in the band, so we duly made a tape. Blackhill made a 'dynamic management decision' to sack a member of the band, delivered by Andrew, who threw in a bit of "Trust me, I've been in this business for years and I tell you he's holding you back musically", and Dave got the sack. In the future somebody explained to me the definition of this tool of dynamic management – it means, simply, fire an expendable member of the group so that the others think you're dynamic. Apparently it will manipuate your band towards respecting and having trust in its management ... What was that Andrew did, the band did what ... fire Dave the bass player - fired?!?!

Just one week before our first tour abroad, when we'd be leaving our management to make deals in our absence we'd been told of one decision that involved sacking Dave, the 'ambitious' one who we'd picked up with Chris from the commune round the corner for our 'one-off' concert all that time ago. Dave, who'd been with us from the very beginning and who'd frozen in the back of the van and starved along with the rest of us since then. Of course, telling him would be down to the Blackhill team but there followed a night of much soul searching and during that evening the band lost a large amount of moral integrity but in the end we went along with the management and Dave was dumped. It was Andrew who phoned Dave to tell him ... he explained how he d'idn't think he was right for the band' ... and though we don't know how Dave took it exactly - apparently he said on the phone, something along the lines of, "If that's what you think ..." it would have been awful to hear - and he still lived in the same house as Chris Wainwright who was still playing with us, well yes but ...

There was an unwritten rule of the road, no women on tour, that is to say, no girlfriends, wives or significant others. This was nothing to do with making sure you had a free hand with any groupies that might appear, it was down to economics and human nature. The economics meant that we couldn't afford to pay for double rooms (in fact, as you'll see, we didn't have any rooms!), and the human nature bit was to do with the fact that some Berts were single and it just seemed like unnecessary boasting to bring your main squeeze out on the road with you. You can imagine our surprise therefore when Dimitri turned up in a newly acquired transit-van to pick us up for our tour of Holland. The look of astonishment on our faces was nothing to do with the fact that we would be travelling in a proper van complete with seats! It was more to do with the fact that sat next to him was his girl friend. There was a row that Dimitri quickly stopped by pointing out that if she couldn't go, he wouldn't go and, more importantly, neither would the PA. It was a fait accompli, and we knew it, but Chris Wainwright was contemptuous and furious to the point where ... he left the band there and then, on the spot, on the pavement outside his house ... and so we had no choice but to head off for the ferry as we contemplated our new line-up. It had already been agreed that Tony Bowers would replace Dave on bass. And with Les absent while he was having treatment we were back to a leaner, fitter, sleak, seven-piece band. We'd be fine, we all agreed as we set off on the tour, and me thinking ...

from swearing never to play in a band again, I was now well and truly embroiled. We'd got a van, we'd got roadies, we'd got a PA. We'd got a London management company, a London agency were getting work for us and it seemed like only a matter of time before we got a record contract. Being so completely 'anti-music' and totally dedicated to the overthrow of what was laughingly known as 'the Rock World', I had to laugh.

AB 1974 - Where's Wally?

5

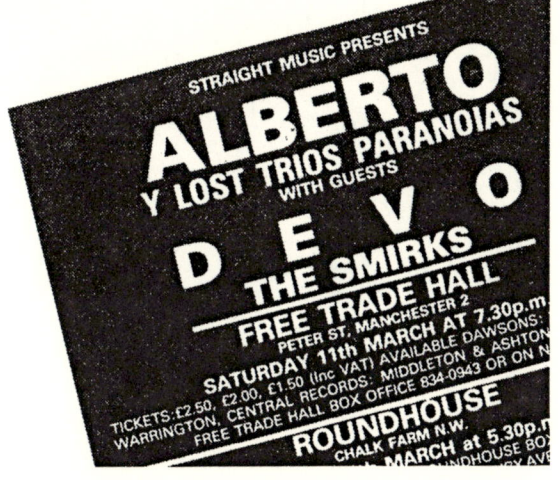

CHAPTER FIVE

CARVING A CAREER IN ROCK

STRAIGHT MUSIC PRESENTS

ALBERTO Y LOST TRIOS PARANOIAS
WITH GUESTS

D E V O
THE SMIRKS

FREE TRADE HALL
PETER ST, MANCHESTER 2
SATURDAY 11th MARCH AT 7.30p.m
TICKETS: £2.50, £2.00, £1.50 (Inc VAT) AVAILABLE DAWSONS:
WARRINGTON, CENTRAL RECORDS: MIDDLETON & ASHTON
FREE TRADE HALL BOX OFFICE 834-0943 OR ON N

ROUNDHOUSE
CHALK FARM N.W.
MARCH at 5.30p.m

W hile we were gallivanting around Europe, back home in Britain, little had changed yet much remained the same. The great Rock 'n' Roll sausage machine trundled on.

Rock music had become so utterly and completely boring that for an outfit like us who gloried in taking the piss out of it all, the whole thing had become as easy as shooting fish in a barrel. Take for example the idea of a 'Rock and Roll Circus'. Now, correct me if I'm wrong but I think the Rolling Stones had already done that in 1967/68. Now, however, Rod Argent decided to stage one at the Roundhouse in Chalk Farm - in 1975! Just look at the advert! It actually has a picture of a clown 'speaking' the words, *ROLL UP, ROLL UP, ALL THE THRILLS OF THE BIG TOP WITH* and there's these elephants adding to the line up of *the Amazing Argent + the inimitable Alberto Y Lost Trios Paranoias* with *PLUS* and *Tight Rope Walkers* and *Trapeze Artist* and *Jugglers*!'

Wow Circus … not.

> **ROUNDHOUSE** CHALK FARM N.W.3
> SUNDAY 13TH APRIL ~ 5·30 ~ 10·30
> STRAIGHT MUSIC PRESENTS
> ★★★ the amazing ★★★
> **ARGENT**
> ★★ the inimitable ★★
> **ALBERTO Y LOST TRIOS PARANOIAS**
> ADM. £1·30 (inc vat) IN ADVANCE R'HOUSE BOX OFF. 267-2564 or LONDON THEATRE BOOKINGS shaft.av.w1. 439-3371 or AT DOOR
> ROLL UP, ROLL UP, ALL THE THRILLS OF THE BIG TOP WITH
> PLUS · Tight Rope Walkers · Trapeze Artiste · Jugglers

The gig started at five-thirty in the evening and we were there nice and early like we'd been told, so we could sound check. If you're second on the bill you have to wait for the headline act to do their check, because of sound balances and equipment placement, etc (if you're third, fourth, or

Carving a Career in Rock 73

fifth, you might have to wait like forever). So we waited. And we waited. We waited first of all for Mr Argent and his boys to show up. Then we waited for Mr Argent and his boys to 'prepare' themselves backstage for their sound check. When they finally ambled on stage you could tell they were 'serious' musicians because they took so long 'gishing', 'scronging', 'thudding', and going 'thump, thump'. For those of you not familiar with musical parlance, these terms were developed by the Berts to refer to, respectively - the cymbals, guitar, bass and bass drum. The words are onomatopoeic, and have been scientifically proven accurate as of going to press.

Anyway, there they were, and there we were, and when they'd finished it was nearly time for the gig to open so, being superstars, they took off so as not to have to mix with the hoi-polloi whilst we did our sound check and sequestered ourselves in the dressing room.

Several 'fans' managed to penetrate our non-existent security cordon and brought us a present of an industrial sized tank of nitrous oxide, laughing gas. To the best of my knowledge I'd never had it before (or since), but it would have been churlish to have rejected this small token of affection. Between bursts of maniacal laughter I can remember being vaguely worried about falling asleep on stage. I needn't have bothered because, shortly after, one of Argent's 'people' came in and asked us to leave the dressing room because Argent wanted it.

GM Backstage somewhere

A quick word about backstage facilities at the Roundhouse. It had one main dressing room that was used to house theatre companies and such like. It would comfortably fit about thirty people. We numbered around ten to a dozen. We figured Argent were smaller. Argent didn't like our response and a team of heavies were sent to despatch us on our way. Not wishing to be beaten to a pulp before we went on, we eventually, begrudgingly made our way to a broom-cupboard, though, I have to admit, because of the nitrous oxide, we couldn't stop laughing as were thrown out.

When our allotted time arrived, we went on stage and did our bit to stem the tide of mediocrity that surrounded us. According to the critics in the papers, we went down a lot better than Argent did. As soon as we'd finished we buggered off, only to discover the next day that Argent had reached the crashing climax of their show and then invited 'their special guests', the Albertos, to join them on stage and join in with whatever piece of crap they were playing. Apparently, Rod Argent faffed around for a bit and then said, "Oh, I think they must have gone home." How right he was.

Giving Good Triple Headers

GM A gas stop on the motorway

Life in the van became more and more hectic as we hurtled around the UK and Europe bringing joy to thousands of deprived punters. Travelling around was pretty primitive back then, fewer motorways and an 'in-house' sound system that could at best be described as 'tinny'. So duff was our cassette player that the only way to pass the endless hours of travelling was by reading. Pete Jenner once told me that we were the best-read band he'd ever come across, and considering that most musicians I ever met thought that 'erudite' was a kind of glue, and 'Sherlock Holmes' a block of flats, he was probably right.

THE NAGS HEAD LONDON ROAD HIGH WYCOMBE
Thursday, August 28th 60p
NUTZ
N/W ALBERTO Y LOST TRIOS PARANOIAS

1975

It was possible back then in the glory days to do 'double-' and sometimes 'triple-headers', that is, two, or three gigs a day. It sounds insane now to even contemplate it, but this is how it could work – Assuming we'd been in Manchester the night before, get up very early and drive as fast as possible to London to play the Friday lunchtime session at the LSE. Then an afternoon break for us (but not the roadies!), and off to play at somewhere like the Marquee in the evening, and then head off to, say, Brunel University for an all-nighter. Our sets lasted, on average, for around ninety minutes and we tended to sweat a lot. We even, at one point, thought of becoming a Soul band and renaming ourselves The Fabulous Perspirations, so drenched were we with our own juices. Stage clothes were kept in a large metal trunk and this led to the creation of what we called 'Tollund Suits', in honour of Tollund Man. This was the poor victim of a ritual sacrifice round about 1500 years ago, whose semi-preserved body had been found at the bottom of a bog in Tollund, Denmark.

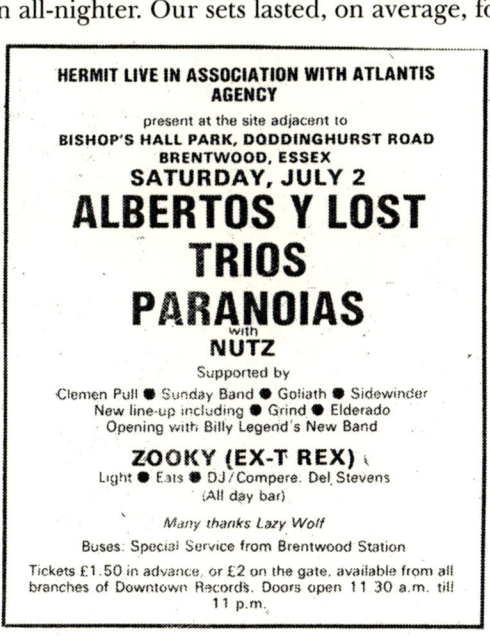

HERMIT LIVE IN ASSOCIATION WITH ATLANTIS AGENCY
present at the site adjacent to
BISHOP'S HALL PARK, DODDINGHURST ROAD
BRENTWOOD, ESSEX
SATURDAY, JULY 2
ALBERTOS Y LOST TRIOS PARANOIAS
with
NUTZ
Supported by
Clemen Pull ● Sunday Band ● Goliath ● Sidewinder
New line-up including ● Grind ● Elderado
Opening with Billy Legend's New Band
ZOOKY (EX-T REX)
Light ● Eats ● DJ / Compere. Del Stevens
(All day bar)
Many thanks Lazy Wolf
Buses: Special Service from Brentwood Station
Tickets £1.50 in advance, or £2 on the gate, available from all branches of Downtown Records. Doors open 11 30 a.m. till 11 p.m.

1976

It was also the title of a book 'The Bog People' – see, I told you we were well read. We were on the move so much that we didn't have time to dry clean our stage wear and consequently the suits grew mouldy inside the trunk and could probably have done the gigs themselves if they'd had an agent.

GM Man without shirt, man without trousers

Another Friday night we topped the bill at Manchester Palace Theatre, flew to Rotterdam first thing in the morning to play at the Pink Pop Festival in Rotterdam in the afternoon, flew back to Stanstead Airport, drove to St Albans and played there in the evening before driving back to Manchester that night. We did pretty much the same thing when we were on at the Reading Festival as the penultimate act on the bill. Headlining was Robin Trower, who Les introduced as 'Percy Thrower', the TV gardener. Les said he knew he was because of all the pot plants back stage and how everybody would 'dig' him. Robin Trower was not amused, but there again, we didn't give a toss what he thought as we had to fly straight back to Holland as soon as we got off stage so we could be on Dutch TV the following night.

We were working our butts off to save Rock from the pit of despond, and what did we get in exchange? Held up at customs usually ...

A Few Quick Words For Touring Groups

If you've ever been in a group (or even travelled in a car!) you'll be familiar with the following problem – asking locals for directions ... The following are all true –

Glasgow. We pulled up at the side of the road and asked a pedestrian -

"Do you know where Sauchiehall Street is?" -

The man stopped - stared at us for a bit and then in best Glaswegian accent snarled - "Aye" and stalked off.

Jim pulled up near Bolton and asked an old chap the way to wherever -

"Aye" said the old man – "Tha should keep right on here until the goostop. Then go left."

"The, er, 'Goostop'?"

"Aye - Goostop ... Tha knows ... Goo ... Stop ... Traffic lights!"

If the person you ask says "You can't miss it from here" - We found that everytime actually you can.

My favourite was a bloke in Leeds who, when we asked him how to get to the local college, said -

"Well, from here you'll need to get the 53 bus" ... That we were sat in a van didn't seem to bother him a bit.

Finally. If you find yourself in a band and you get the inclination to trash somewhere - don't bother. We never did, well once and that came about like this - We were at Nottingham Trent Uni. We were bored in the dressing room when Tony pointed out we'd never trashed a dressing room or a hotel room. We all agreed and mused idly on how one went about it. We decided to do an orderly 'trashing' to see what it would look like. Very carefully we moved the chairs and tables round a bit. Bob suggested that we put one on top of another. After a while we'd built a kind of little pyramid and had just stood back to look at it when one of the University porters popped his head round the door -

"Oh my God!" He shrieked - "You animals! I'm going to tell Mr Frobisher

Putting Trax On Wax

Well, it had to happen, and finally it did. Andrew and Peter managed to broker us a record deal. And the lucky company who were going to throw their tremendous weight behind an all out Alberto assault on the ears of the British public? Why, none other than Indie Folk label, Transatlantic Records. Home to artists as diverse as The Johnstons, Gryphon, Boys of The Lough, and The Young Tradition, I had no qualms about their back catalogue, I just didn't see how we fitted into their great scheme of things. They had a nice office on Marylebone Road, but apart from that - nothing. No studio, no in-house PR team, no designers, and, most importantly, they ran a tight ship financially. That is to say, no parties, no press junkets, not really very much to spend on advertising. In keeping with the times, then as now, the advance we received seemed like a reasonable deal, reasonable enough, that is, when you have nothing anyway. But when you started looking more closely at it, you began to discover the sheer genius of it. We had to pay the studio costs of recording, including the producer and engineer. We also had to pay for the cover design. Frankly I'm surprised we didn't have to pay a percentage to Transatlantic for being on their label - Oh, we did.

P Recording first album, Strawberry Studios

Still, possessed with the arrogance of youth we marched gleefully into Strawberry Studios, 'Home Of The Hits!' and bashed out our first album with Pete Jenner taking the producer's chair. This was quite unusual, normally it was us who took things, normally we'd arrive at a gig and check out what wasn't nailed down. Already in clubs the Visigoths had usually got there before you and there was hardly anything left. But to a dedicated asset stripper there was always something - lightbulbs, toilet rolls, stuff you could just pick up, sorry - 'liberate' - being the White Panther phrase that the Berts so readily adopted. Colleges were another matter. They were a vast cornucopia of delights, armchairs, table lamps, books. I believe there was an enquiry at North London Poly after we'd played there. The Social Secretary got in touch. He wasn't very happy. It appeared that somebody had gone into the Principal's office and taken a huge square of carpet. Not, as you would have thought if the culprit had any wit or cunning about them, from a corner of the room. No, whoever it was, had cut a six foot square from out of the middle of the room with a Stanley knife. Drummers like to mount their drums on carpet so I leave you to draw your own conclusions. Bruce's kitchen for a while was outfitted mainly with motorway service station crockery. Such are the wonders of life, even if the cups were too small for what he charged for a cup of coffee.

Anyway, we cut our first album and tried to make that difficult transition from stage to studio. Comedy is a hard enough thing to get across live. When it's recorded you have to bear in mind that it doesn't very often bear repeated listening. Add to that the fact that we were often challenging the icons of a particular period and you run into even more trouble. Come on, admit it, what's the point of doing a stinging satire on a band like Sailor? Firstly, they did it very well enough themselves. Secondly, who's going to remember them in four years time?

Another hurdle to overcome is naming the first album. We'd been publicising it in the press and onstage as *The Freewheelin' Bob Dylan*, but no-one else, save us and those who got the joke, would go along with it. Plus those wacky, well known comedians who doubled as album designers, Hipgnosis, had a master plan. Best known for their brilliant and inspired work with Pink Floyd and other luminaries of the 'Prog Rock' world, who better to send themselves up than Hipgnosis? If the result (see illustration p79) was designed as some kind of underground act of outrage, to infiltrate the bourgeoisie, then it worked. For about ten minutes. Then chain stores, Boots, WH Smith and Woolworths played it and immediately banned it.

In order to gain maximum publicity somebody at Transatlantic, or Blackhill sent a copy to Mary Whitehouse, leader of the 'clean up Britain' campaign, and she instructed her minions at the Festival of Light to ensure that high-street superstores across the land removed it at once from their shelves. It was great publicity. It also meant that nobody could buy the album. We floundered on.

Italians From Outer Space

For our second foray into the wonderful world of recording (Transatlantic hadn't given up hope yet of having a hit album without the aid of promotion) we decided to 'get back to the country'. Actually, considering the final result maybe I should make that 'get our own back on the country'. Traffic had done it, Eric Clapton had done it, everybody had done it, now it was our turn to pack up our axes and book two weeks in a remote area (equipped with a studio of course) and make music. So off we went to Rockfield Studios in Monmouth, home of Dave Edmunds of *I Hear You Knockin'* fame. It had worked wonders for him and, who knows, maybe it would do the same for us.

I hate the countryside. Andy Warhol said, and I totally agree with him, "In the city you can step into a park if you want trees – In the country – there's nowhere you can step into a city!" But anyway, there we were in the Brecon Mountains, probably, I don't know. Once you've seen on mountain you've seen them all. Dave's place was pretty good though, I have to admit. We were shacked up in a converted farmhouse and the studio was just down the road in the manor house and barn that had once been owned by Sir Henry Royce of Rolls Royce fame. Big deal. Our every whim was catered for. Sessions, engineered by the brilliantly tireless Laurie Latham, went on for ever. The German house engineer told us wonderful stories about Dave Edmunds' recording techniques. Seemed he'd sit himself down at the mixing desk with a jar of Mandrax on top of the console then throw everybody out. Four or five days later they'd come back and the jar would be empty. Dave would be totally unconscious at the desk, but a finished master tape would be resting next to him. Or, more often than not, whirring round and round on the tape deck.

We thought long and hard about Italians, even coming up with the title before we began the sessions. It was, with hindsight, stupid, but we were getting really fed up with Eric Von Daniken type books about extraterrestrials being responsible for everything on the planet, ranging from the pyramids to multi-story car-parks. We decided to throw in our own crack-pot theory – Italians were from outer space. It was easy to prove, the evidence was there for anybody to see – The coliseum was round like a flying saucer and the Pope's hat was shaped like a rocket. The late, great Barney Bubbles produced a sleeve for the album that had a winklepicker shoe's imprint on the moon's surface.

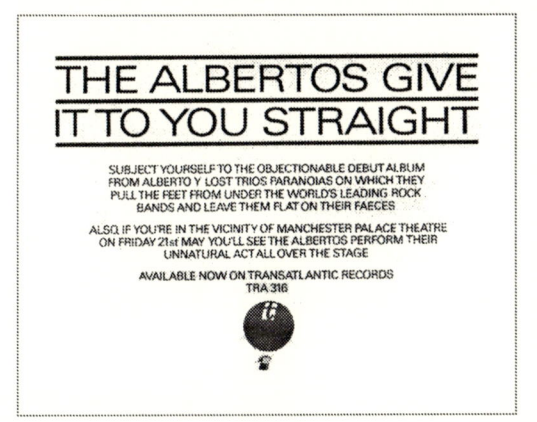

> **THE ALBERTOS GIVE IT TO YOU STRAIGHT**
>
> SUBJECT YOURSELF TO THE OBJECTIONABLE DEBUT ALBUM FROM ALBERTO Y LOST TRIOS PARANOIAS ON WHICH THEY PULL THE FEET FROM UNDER THE WORLD'S LEADING ROCK BANDS AND LEAVE THEM FLAT ON THEIR FAECES
>
> ALSO, IF YOU'RE IN THE VICINITY OF MANCHESTER PALACE THEATRE ON FRIDAY 21st MAY YOU'LL SEE THE ALBERTOS PERFORM THEIR UNNATURAL ACT ALL OVER THE STAGE
>
> AVAILABLE NOW ON TRANSATLANTIC RECORDS
> TRA 316

The whole thing was to have a continuous feel about it, every track linking into the next. We'd even give a nod to our roots by including a brand new comedy script that paid tribute to all our comedy heroes, Hancock, Firesign Theatre, Goons, et al. The whole idea was to make – a concept album! – that creature that we professed to so despise in others. Ours, however, was going to be done properly. Who could fail to note without amusement the myriad cultural references that we'd be throwing up? There was even a Punk Rock track on there for crizake, and it was still only 1976!

In order to ensure that we devoted ourselves entirely to the task in hand we took along with us a bottle full of mescaline. That's when we first noticed Dennis the ten-toed cat.

GM John Cooper Clark for real - note straight hair and clothes - this was 1975

It being the country side and all, we'd had nothing but trouble from creatures all the time we'd been there. The most boring problem was the sheep. Tony and I had gone back to the farm house while the rest of the band were laying down overdubs (man). We tried to open the back door, but couldn't budge it more than half an inch. "Somebody's blocking the door!" shouted Tony. I stiffened in a natural fighting posture that came easily to someone like me who'd existed for years on the fringes of the inner city. "Get out from behind that wall and look through the kitchen window!" he shouted at me. "I'll give you fuckers one second to get away from that door!" he yelled, frightening me to death, but fearing him more than the burglars I sidled up to the window and peeked in.

"It's sheep, Tony," I said … sheepishly. "The kitchen's full of sheep."

And it was. Dozens of them, mooching around as if they hadn't got anything better to do. The back door must have been open and they'd gone in wondering what delights lay in there and once the kitchen was full, the door had been pushed to, they hadn't been able to get back out again. Sheep, so I'm told, are by nature meek and shy. Not this lot. Once we'd managed to force our way in it was like a New Year's sale at Selfridges. They wouldn't budge. Unaware of how much force to use on a sheep, Tony and I started barking like dogs to try and shift them. This just led to more confusion and a general milking around. The more they milled, the harder it was to keep the door wedged open to facilitate their dispersal. By Zeus, I hate sheep.

The barking dogs thing had come to Tony and me quite naturally, because in our feverish minds we were working on the greatest dog album to end all dog albums. Arthur Lee, of Love fame, had recently released a solo album that we had studied very closely. It appeared to be dedicated to dogs. The 'D' string on his guitar was missing, several songs were about dogs, there was 'howling' in the back of one of the cuts. Bob and I thought it would be a great idea to send Arthur a 'message' with our album showing him that we knew where he was coming from. Italians was loaded with 'dog' references. The opening cut was *Old Trust* our anthem to canine infidelity. Dogs barked hither and yon throughout many of the tracks, and we tried to play as many of them in the key of 'D' as we could reasonably get away with. Laurie Latham hadn't batted an eyelid when we told him of our cunning masterplan – When we mastered the final cut of the album we got him to place a super high pitched whine that only dogs would hear. This would make them bark throughout the playing of the album, assuming that any of our fat, bearded fans had dogs.

> **C. P. Lee,** self-styled 'very funny man' knocked together an almost perfect impersonation of fellow Mancunian **John Cooper Cluck** in honour of their John's headline appearance at a certain Hammersmith Poetry Feast. The only way you could tell the difference was by observing that Cluck does not in fact have a dog on his head . . .

If any of you try and check this out and you haven't got the vinyl version of the album, only the CD, you may be a little disappointed. When it was re-mastered for digital transfer the engineers thought the 'doggy noise' was a mistake and took it off. Now your dogs will only bark because they think the album sucks.

But, Dennis, I hear you ask, what of Dennis? ... Right. It being a farm there were lots of feral cats living there. You could look but you couldn't touch. They didn't go for humans very much. Who, frankly, can blame them? One of them however, presumably in search of rodent fodder, had chased some bit of wild-life into the studio. It had looked around and dug the vibes. 'Dennis' as we immediately christened him, decided to take up residence for the duration of the album. A big, buggering farm cat, Dennis was. The kind of cat who took no gruff when him strut his stuff. Very late at night, or more precisely, early in the morning, when we were sat listening to playbacks of the days work, Dennis might, possibly might, deign to come over and curl up in your lap, in which case you were highly honoured. He didn't spread his fleas with just anybody.

Otto, the German engineer was very impressed. "Zey don't like humans," he told us in awe and wonder at our Grizzly Adam's like hold over the feral feline. "You should be honoured. Zey are very inbred you know". Tony had just discovered that and let out a shriek that sent Dennis scurrying from his lap.

"He's got ten fucking toes! Tony shouted.

"Fuck off. That's impossible. He wouldn't be able to walk." I said.

For some strange reason, Otto said, "No, no. Zat gives him extra grip on ze ice."

For obvious reasons this stopped all further discussion. A few minutes later Dennis crept back in and settled on my lap.

Gingerly I counted his toes, hoping he wouldn't know I was looking ...

"Ten alright." I said to the room.

"Fucking hell!" everyone replied.

Skite

'Skite' is a word that survived in English until near the end of the 19th century. It meant 'Shit', and I wanted an album called that to point out the idiocy of censorship that says one word is correct and another obscene. Essentially, it meant that words don't possess anything unless society imposes a meaning on them. When I listen to it now, I believe it's an album that's got some great songs and performances on it. Musically, it's certainly the best thing we produced. But it's a long time ago now and the last thing the world needs is more music, so unless your curiosity is particularly piqued ...

Two tracks on the album in particular summed up that period - *Can You Hear Me Mother Superior* - 'I think I've lost my mind - Oh No! There it is on the chair where I left it, I only borrowed it, It wasn't actually mine.' and *God Is Mad* featuring Roger Ruskin Spear on tenor/saxophone. I was really determined to get the Bonzos involved in some way or another with

Albertos - Ruskin Spear was the only one we could get to come and record with us at the time. He played three different solos in three different styles and I did the usual 'can't decide what to do' trick of putting them altogether instead of using just one. It was the soundtrack for *Skite* the stage show that was going our follow up to *Sleak* and *Never Mind The Bullocks*. Centred around a TV chat show that's hijacked by terrorists. Peter Cook said Skite was one of the funniest things he'd ever read, but sadly it never got produced ... more on all this in the final chapter entitled *The Curse Of The Berts*.

Snuff Rock

Ah, *Snuff Rock*. This has indeed got an entire chapter (8) to itself, but the story of the recording of the soundtrack is a great example of what real Rock 'n' Roll should be all about.

We knew exactly what we were doing with the four tunes that were the climax of *Sleak* the show. They were a pastiche, parody, call it what you will, of the prevailing mood of the moment. In terms of what was going down musically, as contemporary pieces, they were the best thing musically that the Berts ever did, solid, level and in front. What's been worrying ever since, is how many people took them seriously. As if those particular songs about urban angst and suicide were real! Punk Rock, eh? My dear, the smoke, the noise - and the people!

Performing them night after night meant that by the time we went into the studio we had them honed to perfection. Somehow, bless 'em, Andrew and Peter managed to persuade Transatlantic to let us off our contract and go with Stiff records. The whole Punk thing was exploding and Stiff were at the forefront of the whole kit and caboodle what with the Damned and Elvis Costello. Sharing the same building as them obviously helped too.

Jake Rivera and Dave Robinson, founder/owners of Stiff Records, were open to the idea. They'd seen the show and loved it. They got the joke, and both of them dug that any record from Sleak had to be on Stiff, no bones about it. There was also only one person in the entire world who could produce it and that was Nick Lowe. Nick and I had been pootling around anyway and Jake was forever pumping me for ideas about outrages that we could commit, so it was really an accident that was waiting to happen.

During the run of Sleak, we took a Sunday evening off and turned it into a recording session at the Work House studios owned by Manfred Mann. We went in at mid-day and left at mid-night, having cut and mastered four tracks, *Snuffin' Inna Babylon,* the Reggae tribute to John Lydon's Jamaican obsession; *Snuffin' Like That,* with its contentious life-affirming line – 'council estate, filled with hate, gonna end it now 'fore it's too late!'; the self explanatory *Kill,* and finally, perhaps the Albertos' greatest song, *I'm Gobbing On Life.* It was on this number that Nick showed his particular ear for the exemplary when he suggested to Simon 'Tommy' White, that the lead break should explode in a crescendo of feedback. That's the way Simon played it and it's still brilliant to this very day.

P (L-R) Nic Lowe, Bob Harding, Simon Tommy White recording Snuff

Snuff Rock came out on Stiff a few weeks later and became a best seller on their catalogue, shifting, eventually, so I'm told, over 25,000 units. It's still played today, whether as a 'real' Punk item, or as a novelty, depends on who's at the turntable. Tracks get used for film soundtracks and TV shows. If only they'd use it as an advert for Levis and we could all retire.

The Emperor's New Music

During my tenure with the Berts I'd occasionally undertake little musical outrages whenever possible. The whole concept of 'Indie' music was very appealing. All across the country bands were putting out their own stuff on their own labels. Manchester had led the way with Buzzcocks's *Spiral Scratch* and Slaughter's *Cranked Up Really High* on Tosh's Rabid label. There had to be an opportunity somewhere for us/or me, to exploit the propagandist purposes of the medium? In conversations with Martin, I became even more convinced that there was now even more reason for this 'fight back'. Kicking holes in the façade of Rock was deeply appealing and knocking out some 'guerilla' recordings gave me a chance to vent off some of the frustration I felt about our recording career.

Rabid was doing really well at the time and Tosh Ryan gave Lawrence Beadle the green light to go ahead with an off-shoot label called Absurd, to release material that defied categorisation as either Punk, New Wave, or even Novelty. Albertos member, John Scott dived in first with *Snap It Around* by 48 Chairs. Then he joined forces with Captain Mog and they released material as Bet Lynch's Legs. Next up was my duo with John, Gerry and The Holograms. The next thing we knew it was being played by John Peel, and Frank Zappa had chosen it as one of his all-time top twenty records (along with two more featuring John Scott). If anyone should have tried out for the Mothers it was him!

Flushed with success, John and I plotted further outrages. *A Day In The*

Life Of A House, was going to be a 24 hour long recording of the activities in somebody's house, speeded up to fit in a three and a half minute format with a drum machine backing. Sadly, this never saw the light of day. Neither did *Charlie The Cheeseplant*. We discovered that you could rig plants up to electronic devices that emitted beeps and squawks. Now, what if you recorded those noises and gave them a backing track? We fantasised about a publicity campaign – photographs of a cheeseplant in the back of a limo surrounded by adoring groupies – a cheeseplant on stage, in front of a microphone – Fortunately for the world that's all we did, fantasise, but Gerry and The Holograms did carry out one more attack on the Rock business – *The Emperor's New Music*.

Picture discs, metal boxes, limited editions, it was all getting out of hand, and what had, in 1972, felt like preposterous pretentiousness, was beginning to look like naïve, innocent fumbling compared to the excesses of the new decade. It was time to strike back with the world's first unplayable single! Absurd announced the release of Gerry and The Hologram's *The Emperor's New Music*, a very limited edition picture disc and the orders came flooding in! We told them it was unplayable. We even made doubly sure of that by gluing them inside the sleeve, but still they wanted them. There wasn't really very much you could do after something like that, so we more or less gave up.

GM Above and opposite - ALBERTOS - by any means necessary

Carving a Career in Rock 89

ALBERTO Y LOST TRIOS PARANOIAS

CHAPTER SIX

6

PLAYING FOR THE STONED HEADS OF EUROPE

STRAIGHT MUSIC PRESENTS

ALBERTO Y LOST TRIOS PARANOIAS
WITH GUESTS

D E V O
THE SMIRKS

FREE TRADE HALL
PETER ST, MANCHESTER 2
SATURDAY 11th MARCH AT 7.30p.m.
TICKETS: £2.50, £2.00, £1.50 (Inc VAT) AVAILABLE DAWSONS: WARRINGTON, CENTRAL RECORDS: MIDDLETON & ASHTON, FREE TRADE HALL BOX OFFICE 834-0943 OR ON N

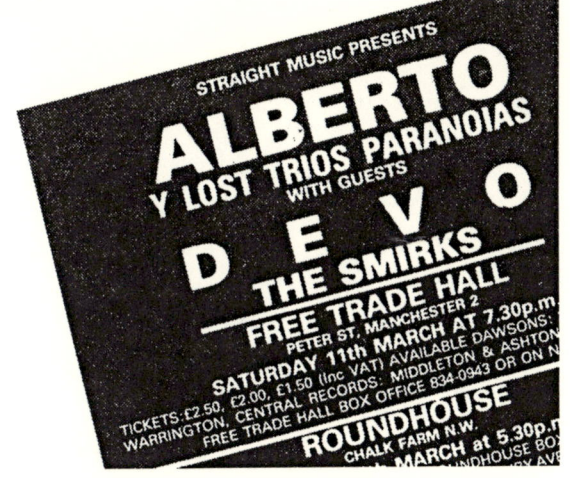

ROUNDHOUSE
CHALK FARM N.W.
MARCH at 5.30p.m.

I still find it somewhat strange that the Berts were so popular in Europe. Considering that such a large percentage of the act relied on verbals, and that those particular verbals were in English (of sorts). But popular we were, so popular in fact that by 1976 we spent more time touring there than we did at home. In the space of a few months, we went from playing 'Youth Centres' like Der Hippo in Leeuwarden to concert halls and festivals all across the Lowlands and Germany - and we also did lots of radio and TV there too. Why we were on so often eluded us at the time as well. Because we couldn't usually understand what the MCs were saying when they introduced us we came to the conclusion that they were using us as a kind of public service announcement about the dangers of drugs - Kind of, "Look kids. This is what can happen to you if you shovel shit up your beaks." Or, "Drugs! - Just say Alberto!"

We'd only toured Belgium once when Andrew said to us that we'd been booked for an election night special on Belgium TV. What? An election night special? It was true. We got to the TV station in Brussels and were plonked into a studio that had been set up like a nightclub. Tables with candles stuck in wine bottles, chairs, a little stage with curtains, lots of smoke to give it atmosphere, and an audience of bored looking members of the public. Not freaks, ordinary 'civilians'. Middle-aged and looking distinctly uncomfortable. Just one question - What the Hell had all this got to do with a general election? Seemed that us and a bunch of Belgian satirists, fire-eaters and magicians were the light relief. In a studio opposite, the Belgium equivalent of Peter Snow would step back from his 'Swingometer', and say -

Genuine fun turns obscene

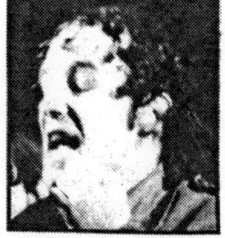

■ ALBERTO Y LOS TRIOS

I RECENTLY saw Albertos Y Los Trios Paranoias for the second time. The first time I saw them they were genuinely funny, and were on this occasion for the first 20 minutes or so. The act then came a little repetitive and the closing part of the show was so obscene it was embarrassing for all present.
  There's no need to include this mindless vulgarity, and if the Albertos persist with this act they will soon find themselves just as much an institution of half-empty students as many of the acts they choose to satirize. — Dave Foley, Wolverhampton.

"And while we wait for the results from Liege to come in, let's go over to our election nightclub and have another number from those irascible rascals from England, Alberto Y Lost Trios Paranoias!" - and we'd belt into *Jesus Wept*, or some other outrage against musical sanity. Belgium might be quite small, but it was a long night waiting for all those results to come in, and half way through the evening another thought crossed our minds - As this was the State channel, and it was the election programme, it was odds on that the King would be watching at home in his palace – Brilliant! Another outrage perpetrated on an unsuspecting public.

Radio Free Dope and The Masked Avenger

Holland's more relaxed attitude to soft drugs is well known, but it still came as a surprise to us when we arrived there for the first time in 1975. Whilst not as widespread as the 'cafés' are now, there were still plenty of spaces in which cannabis was condoned, consumed and, even, positively encouraged. What very quickly blew our minds (and I'm not talking about Nepalese Temple Ball) was a Dutch radio station that may have been called VPRO, but we nicknamed, 'Radio Free Dope'. This was an official, licensed radio station, kind of the Dutch equivalent of the BBC. What set it apart from Lord Reith's concept of 'public service broadcasting' was the kind of public that they thought they were broadcasting to. That is, Heads, Freaks, Dopers, Satanists, whatever.

VPRO was a wonderful legacy of the glorious days of the Provos (Dutch radical 'provocateurs' who brought about much social change in the 1960s) and provided a wonderful blend of eclectic programming. Concerts by the latest groups, killer record shows with top-notch, very hip DJs, and, best of all, a weekly 'dope market report', brought to you by the son of a Dutch Government Minister. This programme went out, if I recall correctly, on a Friday evening and gave a very detailed account of what brands of hash had recently arrived in Amsterdam, what

P (L-R) Bob, Gorden Kaye, Tony, CP

quality they were, and what price you should pay for them. It also gave pharmacological reports on the quality, strength and purity of the LSD currently available.

We did lots of shows for them, live and pre-recorded. We also did a heap of gigs for the station in the Vondel Park in the middle of Amsterdam. These were free concerts which were recorded for later transmission. There was one in particular which must have caused the radio audience at home to be more than somewhat perplexed. It was a warm, sunny, Sunday afternoon and we'd driven overnight from Germany. We parked behind the stage and met up with a bunch of our Dutch (and English) friends. It is possible that by mistake, we imbibed certain substances of an herbal nature. Many of our gigs in Holland felt like we were wading

Vondel Park, Amsterdam, just before the bee attack

through treacle, which I tend to put down to 'transit lag', or language differences.

Anyway, we took to the stage and the set began quite normally. Jimmy had caroused his way through *Old Trust*, and we were happily ploughing our way through the complex, but exciting dance routines demanded by *Teenage Paradise*, when, all of a sudden, I couldn't hear the band. I could hear something though. I could hear screaming and cursing, followed by a loud 'CRASH!'. I turned round and watched, as if in slow-motion, all the guitar amplifiers collapse into one another like a row of dominoes. These dominoes then fell into the drum riser, which shuddered and then disappeared under a heap of Marshall amps and crashing cymbals. Bruce rose from the debris, haughty and imperious, then turned red and had an asthma attack. Simon and Tony lay in a growling heap on the floor, hopelessly entangled in guitar leads and Fenders. Doug Marnoch, the roady, ran on stage and valiantly attempted to disentangle musicians from equipment. It was a daunting task, one that he was ill-equipped for, having also accidentally imbibed 'things'. He began laughing and sat in a heap on the stage. The audience looked at us for a few moments and

ALBERTO Y LOST TRIOS PARANOIAS

Can you see the bee?

then began to tentatively applaud, assuming that the on-stage debacle was part of the act. Under cover of this applause I sidled up to Tony and asked what had happened.

"Bee!" he hissed.

"I am." I said, eerily echoing a Neil Diamond song.

"A fucking bee! Tried to sting me!"

It all became clear. The errant insect had intruded upon Tony's personal space. He'd taken evasive action which resulted in him becoming wrapped up in his guitar lead. He'd slipped in his efforts to escape the deadly attack and ended flat on his ass watching in horrified disbelief as everything came tumbling down.

We took a short break while the roadies set all the gear up again, but it was too late, the damage had been done and we never recovered equilibrium. The audience must have been more stoned than we were because at the end they shouted for an encore. I brought the bee back on.

Sailing Through The Milky Way

Our first ever gig in Holland was at Der Hippo in Leeuwarden, a club typical of the model that was being developed around the Netherlands at the time. More arts lab than 'youth centre', it was equipped with a coffee bar/bar, a performance room and, what would be now known as, a chill out room. Other places which were bigger had cinemas, experimental theatres, even book stores. It was a gig we were to return to again and again. That first time though introduced me to the cultural chaos and confusion that passed for Europe – "You're not in Kansas anymore, Toto" – should have been uppermost in my mind when a very attractive girl who'd been watching us bring the gear in (yes, we all helped Dimitri back then. He was very sensitive) came and sat next to me – "Would you like a shag?" she asked innocently – "But we've only just met," I answered ha ha, knowing that she was offering me her tobacco. There were loads of linguistic bantering to be had in Holland but I won't bother going into the rest, suffice to say that they had to do with mishearing words like 'fork' and, "I make a great breakfast." On with the story, less of the cheese.

This gig in Leeuwarden set the scene for the rest of our career in the Netherlands. We went out onto the stage and started playing our standard set. After the first number, the audience reaction was zero - nothing. They just sat there and looked at us. We figured, "Oh well, it must be the language barrier. What idiot booked us on a Dutch tour anyway?" We battled on. We threw everything we could at the audience who steadfastly refused to do anything but sit there. We went beyond the bounds of any known Albertos' set and pushed the envelope of Comedy Rock to its limits. Even Bruce's drum solo failed to elicit any noticeable reaction. It felt like it was turning into a gigantic disaster, like Christmas wasn't far away and we were the turkey on the table. When the set finished with its obligatory explosion, we walked off to the dressing room dejectedly.

A few moments later the guy who ran the gig came running in – "What are you doing?" he shouted. "They want more!"

We stuck our heads out of the door and it was true. The audience were going as apeshit as I've ever seen the Dutch go (which obviously wasn't much as this was the first time I'd ever seen a Dutch audience), whooping and hollering and stamping their feet for an encore. We

℗ 1977 Not Elvis Costello & Judy Lloyd, Rotterdam

simply couldn't believe it. There'd been no reaction at all while we'd been playing and spieling our best gags for the last hour and a half, and now you would have thought that Eric Clapton and Jimi Hendrix were there and they wanted MORE! We were used to drunken adulation, but stoned adulation was a new one on us. So of course, ever the gentlemen, we obliged and loped back on stage in a strange kind of muted, or muffled, glory, because we weren't quite certain what was going down, and then rocked them to the rafters again.

As the tour progressed we got the same reception every night – the audience would move from quiet, polite attentiveness during the show, to mad screaming out for more at the end. Kind of like they didn't want to wear themselves out or something. When we talked to other British bands on the circuit they reported exactly the same thing.

In Amsterdam, it was even freakier. Perhaps the dope was stronger? In the 'Melkweg' (Milky Way), which was to become virtually our second home, the concert room had a huge raised dais covered with mattresses and sheets of foam rubber which the audience could lie on as the effects of the Melkweg's legendary 'Space Cake' took effect.

PARANOIAS PUNCH-UP!

ALBERTO y Lost Trios Paranoias were involved in an incident in Holland last weekend when, following a riot-torn concert in Rotterdam, they were set upon by a gang of youths in a near-by restaurant. Fortunately the band proved capable of giving more than they received, and seven of their attackers were subsequently taken to hospital for treatment. Alberto's only casualty was lead singer C. P. Lee, who sustained a broken nose. The Dutch police said they would not be prefering any charges against the band, because they had been "severely provoked".

A momentary digression. A bunch of friends in Amsterdam held a party for us once, on one of our nights off. We arrived at the apartment where it was being held, and helped ourselves to the delicious looking cake that was laid out with the drinks and stuff. It was a space cake with a difference – As well as the usual half a pound of dope that had been mixed in with it, some bright spark had thought to add a layer of icing made out of amphetamine sulphate. The result was that within an hour or so, the Berts were lying totally blitzed on the floor, completely incapable of any movement yet utterly alert and all babbling incoherently about the time they were seven and saw an ant walk across the back door step and how it had changed the way they looked at things if it hadn't been for the fact that a sparrow always reminded them of the time that woman on TV had said that ... Oh well, I guess you get the picture.

We became more popular in Holland and returned again and again. The first time there we had no money and slept on floors in what were known as 'sleep-ins', hippy crash pads for penniless teen tourists. Our diet was limited to 'frites' (chips), usually with mayonnaise, though my particular favourite was peanut sauce. With our success came proper hotels and a diet rich in exotic delights such as the hilariously named 'Nasi Goreng' and 'Bami Goreng' (Indonesian curry platters with fried eggs on top). We also got regular residencies at the larger venues such as the Melkweg and Der Eksit in Rotterdam. These places still held the 1960s ethos of the UK 'arts labs', and we'd find ourselves booked for two weeks or so as part of things like the *Festival of Fools*, or Rottterdam's *International Sci Fi Festival*. The events spilled out into public spaces all over the cities and it's at this time we first came across wonderful performers of street theatre such as the John Bull Puncture Repair Kit, The Phantom Captain, and The Crystal Theatre.

Our first encounteer with the Crystal Theatre was when they were mounting a two-day mountaineering expedition to climb the steps of Rotterdam's central post-office. They started off by establishing base camp, and then, complete with Sherpas and guides, cramponed and glissaded their way to the PO front doors, sleeping at night in little tents perched precariously halfway up the steps. All ten of them. These people were great to hang out with and their street-theatre anarchy more than matched our anarchic musical approach.

Such shit-hot theatricality provided brilliant spectacles for the Berts and who can forget John Bull's twenty-one herring salute on the Dutch queen's official birthday. Not me - All the local civic dignitaries were invited to witness this show of affection. They gathered together outside De Lantaaren arts house and solemnly watched as twenty-one dead herrings stuffed with charges were exploded in sequence. Then a man dressed in white robes rode by on a horse shouting – "More sugar!"

Surrounded by this lot of maniacs, we did our best to ensure that chaos reigned whenever possible. One night at the Melkweg, after what felt like an interminable wait while a Japanese theatre company bored the audience (and us) rigid with their version of Titus Andronicus, performed not only in Japanese, but also in the nude (and without props), Les decided to take action. We'd been scheduled to go onstage at nine. It was now 10.15 and Les marched out on stage - during one of the actor's monologues.

Moving right to the front of the stage Les shouted to the audience – "Do you want this load of bollocks!?" He pulled his pants down – "Or this load of bollocks?!" and within fifteen minutes we were on stage, with Les continuing his entire act in the nude.

"Ich Bin Ein Hamburger!"

Germany and Belgium gigs were not nearly as laid back as the Netherlands, if you catch my drift. We were used to going on stage way after nine o'clock but with the exception of Brussels, we were shocked to find that we were expected on stage at seven thirty, sometimes earlier. The smell

P 1978 Mucking about in Rotterdam

of tear gas at one of our first Belgian concerts alerted us to the fact that there was a curfew in place because of student rioting. We played in a lecture theatre and the audience sat at desks. Riot police surrounded the university. It was awful and there was bugger all to do back then in Brussels except wish you were in Amsterdam. No matter where you played in Belgium, with the early concert start time and with it being such a small country, playing so early meant that we were often back in our Brussels hotel before mid-night.

Germany, on the other hand, did offer after-hours entertainment, but not necessarily the kind you wanted. The first time we played there was at a club in Hamburg on the infamous Reeperbahn. On the six or seven times we played there, the promoter put us in the same hotel down the street from the gig. He thought it had character. We thought we'd get killed. We were there on New Year's Eve in 1975 and had a night off. We thought we'd go for a walk. It was like something out of Dante's Inferno. Topless prostitutes lunged out from doorways, shrieking and waving bottles of champagne. Fireworks exploded all around our feet. We actually had to step over a body which was dumped conveniently at the

P Bruce's reflection of Jamie Oliver is uncannily prescient.

entrance to the police headquarters - I was shocked when I saw several policemen ignoring the body and stepping over it too. A group of drunks chased me down the street shouting that they hated Arabs. Now of course Manchester city centre's like that every weekend night, but in those times it was the only place in the world I'd seen behaviour like that.

The next night the club management demanded that we played four 45-minute sets. When it came time for Bruce's drum solo we'd gone through every trick in the Berts' book to try and get a laugh, but with hardly any success. The German audience just stared at us like we were from another planet. Bruce hammered away for a while then spoke quite slowly to them. As he spoke he kept up a constant rhythm on his kit.

"That was a parradiddle." He said.

"That was a double parradiddle." He continued, doubling his diddles.

"Here's a sound you'll probably all recognise," he added, changing the beat slightly, "It's a Lancaster bomber!" He began pounding his tom-tom.

"And here's another one!"

This was Hamburg, probably one of the most bombed cities in Europe during the war. We looked at the audience. They were open mouthed in disbelief. We weren't moving either, we'd frozen and were looking for the nearest exit for a hasty retreat ... Bruce still hammering away. Then the strangest thing happened. They started laughing. Then they laughed some more and started applauding.

GM Berts let rip in music mash-up

"This one's for Tosh!" Bruce shouted. Tosh's dad had been killed during the war ("Yeah, robbing a fucking bank." Anon.).

Tony Tyler, the NME journalist, was in the audience and later that night he said it was one of the funniest things he'd seen in his life. And we all mused, funny people the Germans.

Take our German promoter Martin Salamans for instance – An affable chap who was taking a risk putting us on in Germany, but he'd seen how well we'd gone down in the Lowlands and thought it was worth a shot. He also thought that the Albertos would act as a babe magnet and he would be surrounded by beautiful Rhine Maidens or whatever. We were the Albertos and bizarre as it is to reflect on what might be perceived as the Glory Years of sex 'n' drugs 'n' rock'n' roll, the people we usually attracted backstage were fat blokes with beards who wanted to talk about Monty Python or the Goons. Goons yes – girls no. This didn't put Martin off. When it finally dawned on him that this was not to be a Bacchanalian orgy across the Fatherland he started chatting up - how would Bruce have put it? – 'owt with an handbag' – because he had a theory that he was forever telling us ... "If you want a woman you must look for the older one – if they are 30 or more, biologically they must be having it!'

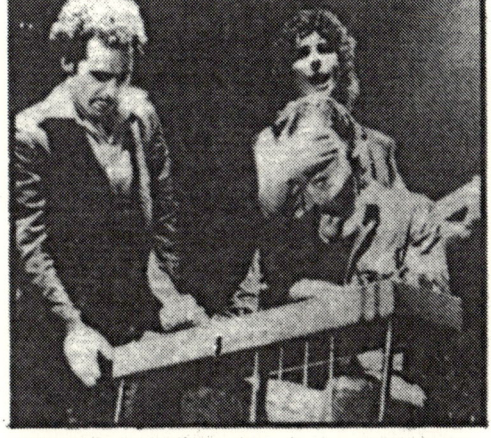

ALBERTO Y Lost Trios Paranoias provide the all-too-serious world of rockpop with a much-needed shot of humour at Bath University (Friday), Sheffield Top Rank (Sunday), Oldham Civic Hall (Monday).

Strange times indeed. Once, having checked into our hotel room in Berlin, Tony and I were startled by the porter (who for some reason was dressed in a white nurses-style tunic) locking us in our room. We hammered on the door until someone let us out and we ran downstairs to get the hell out of the hotel. As we went downstairs we did a double-take – Bruce was manning the hotel switchboard! He looked quite fetching in a vintage headset and he waved as we checked out at the desk ... Bruce was staying, but we were out of there. I still haven't figured that whole episode out yet.

Andrew King and I had been invited to have lunch with the director and producer of German TV's biggest Rock show, *Rockpalast*. "We're not sure the band would be right for our kind of programme," Christian the show's director said and before Andrew could say anything, I dived in. "Absolutely right," I agreed, "Your format's too conventional for us." Andrew looked fit to choke on his pheasant. *Rockpalast* was a simple 'in-concert' style show and fine for regular 'music' bands. We weren't. "But give us a budget and two days in the studio and I'll come up with a script that'll win you the Golden Rose of Montreux award." I blagged.

So it was a month or so later we found ourselves in WDR studios in Cologne recording a show that when I watch it now, I can't believe was made, let alone aired. Throughout the programme selections from the Koran, in Arabic, ran along the bottom of the screen. German TV's top sports presenter introduced the show, describing the fabulous moves we'd be making and how close we were to winning the Cup. The first half consisted of a series of sketches in which various members of the band did strange things in a variety of natty costumes. Teams of female disco dancers shrugged and boogied their way through our Barry White parody, *I'll Come If You Let Me*. Bob sang in French to a gigantic snail. Most bizarre of all was a number featuring Jimmy, Bob and I, in Black-face, wearing lederhosen and Alpine hats yodelling a Soul number. The second half was shot in front of a live audience (I hate it when they're dead, don't you?), and was more or less our standard set, complete with eccentric dancing, incomprehensible puns in 'Euro-speak', and the traditional explosion. The blag had worked well, though obviously it didn't win any TV awards, being just too weird.

Somewhere in a Bavarian forest a group of American musicians called Devo were taking a break from rehearsing. By chance they came upon our episode of *Rockpalast* as it was being broadcast. This was to result in them writing a song called *Too Much Paranoias*. Although when they supported us in England a few months later, they had no idea we were the same people they'd seen on TV - they thought that had been a strange bunch of German musicians!

I am told that WDR occasionally repeats the programme, no doubt as a warning to kids about the dangers of drugs.

Fucking With Ted Nugent

We started getting booked for festivals all over Europe, some gigantic ones down in Southern Germany, Pink Pop in Holland, Midnight Sun in Finland – Les, "I just love Finnish cooking ... the way you do eggs. - how do you manage to fry them 'til the shell's so crunchy and black?" Ones in Switzerland – Les, "Your toilets here are so clean I've just eaten my dinner out of one".

We arrived at one three-day long smorgasbord of musical delights and settled into our caravan in the backstage area. The drink was flowing nicely and we were entertaining guests from Irish band Horslips who were also on the bill. Headlining was American gun/guitar freak Ted Nugent, who was in the next caravan to us. Nugent's reputation was built on his heroic efforts in bringing wailing feedback to the masses. He'd become so involved in 'giving his all' to his playing that a roady had to run on every now and again and give him oxygen so he could keep on playing. The high point of his set was climaxing in a crescendo of blazing guitar pyrotechnics and turning to face his amp, on which was placed a large glass fish bowl. He would then shatter the bowl through the awesome power of his playing.

Horslips and the Berts weren't very impressed with Mr Nugent. From within his caravan came the harsh sound of him warming up. We'd already been on stage and so had Horslips. We'd also drunk lots of Bavarian beer and were feeling quite convivial. Tony plugged his Fender into his practice amp and started matching Nugent note for note. Nugent's playing got more and more flashy. So did Tony's. Rough Irish voices joined the Berts in shouts of encouragement to "Our Man! – Go on now! Beat the trousers off him!" Nugent's guitar went silent, and a few moments later there was a knock on our caravan door. I opened it and stood outside was one of his roadies.

Roady - "Shut that fuckin' noise off - Ted's practising."

Me - "Sounds like he fucking needs to." and I withdrew quickly back into the caravan - Tony carried on ...

A few more minutes later and a gentleman introducing himself as Ted's manager came across and told us that Ted was top of the bill and if we knew what was good for us we should "shut the fuck up, Limey assholes". Before Horslips could protest that they were Irish, he added, "And that goes for you too, you fucking Micks."

A short while later, and we and Horslips all silently trouped out to the stage area to watch his set, our hearts filled with black thoughts of vengeance. To a tape of *America The Beautiful* and flanked by a Marine Corps guard of honour in full dress uniform, Nugent strode onto the stage and proceeded to play. Off he went into guitar-solo wonderland. On came roadies to give him oxygen. On he played. And on. Then came the bowl shattering bit and we watched from the side of the stage as he turned to face his amp and, half crouching, blasted a wall of feedback at it. What the audience couldn't see, stooping, just behind the amp, was the roady who'd come to our caravan. He was holding a little hammer. When Ted's histrionic facial expressions reached maximum overload and the wailing guitar had gone beyond the pain threshold, the roady tapped the bowl. It shattered to the cheers of the audience. Nugent collapsed in a triumphant heap on the stage as the crowd went wild.

We trudged back towards the caravans. Horslips looked at their battered transit van. We looked at our beloved weather-beaten VW micro-bus. Then we all looked at Ted Nugent's gigantic Mercedes Benz limo. "Time we were off now, lads," said one of Horslips. "Indeed," said we. "Just one more thing before we go," they added. "Indeed," we replied. Two of them went on one side of the limo and crouched down. Two of us did the same on the opposite side ... the limo sank lower as the air left its tyres. We bade each other good bye and drove off into the night.

A Session With Freud

One of our European highlights has to be a two-week residency in an abattoir in Vienna. Thankfully, the abattoir had been converted into a venue, but the smell still lingered. Because we were living in Vienna for the duration we put ourselves out a bit, even getting free admission to an after-hours club and causing Austrian brewery shares to sky-rocket. We could do the tourist thing - get out and about, take in the sights - and what sights they were.

When you're in a band the most you generally get to see of anywhere is the view through the van windows as you drive in, then the interior of some dreadful club, then your hotel room until the next morning when you get to see the view of the city you saw coming in again as you drive out again to the next gig. Les, not surprisingly considering his state, was always begging us to take a detour so we could look at some monument or other. My biggest thrill was going round foreign supermarkets. To me, the explained so much about other cultures that guide books never could. I found out that you could buy bottles of baked beans in Holland! That the German hausfrau favoured coloured clotheslines! That the average Belgian supermarket had more gourmet delights at the deli counter than possibly all the specialist shops in Manchester put together!

Anyway, our cultural trawl through Vienna took us to an Andy Warhol exhibition in the State Museum, which also housed the (in)famous Spear of Longinius (Destiny) that allegedly pierced Christ's side on the cross.

Playing for the Stoned Heads of Europe   107

Subsequently used as a talisman of power by the Emperor Charlamagne, and then the House of Hapsburg for the next seven hundred years, it was seized by Hitler during the Austrian Anschluss. The Americans took possession of it at the end of the Second War and returned it to Austria where it still resides in the Hapsburg museum. Obviously, this artefact was high on our list of 'must see' priorities ...

To a man, the Albertos harboured a long felt and deep interest in the machinations of the Holy Roman Empire, so a chance to see one of its prize possessions, one that had actually been fondled by Ludwig of Bavaria, was not to be missed. We trouped down into the basement to look at the Spear of Destiny - great cultural influence that it is - Kirk Brandon had read the same book as us – *The Spear of Destiny* - hence his band's name. The book was written by Trevor Ravenscroft. - and his son played the saxaphone on Gerry Rafferty's Baker Street (if you ever need to know for a pub quiz!).

To have seen Warhol's Skulls and a highly-charged occult artefact, the Spear, all in one day, was mind-blowing enough. So imagine how far-blasted into the fargonesphere we were spun when a suited-straight-type guy walked up to us as we left the building ... and said, as he handed us a small packet, "You'll be wanting these." We opened the it as he walked away and were astonished to find postcards of the spear. Weird shit.

Another Viennese whirl was our visit to Freud's house. There was his couch on which he'd developed his theories about psycho-analysis. There were his little Ancient Egyptian figurines that tapped in to the universal unconsciousness. And there on the

P Vienna 1979 Simon and Bruce in a scene from The Third Man

mantelpiece was an empty space ... Instead of what the catalogue of items stated would be on view – 'a bottle of cocaine as would have been used by Dr Freud', was a note that read – 'This exhibit has been removed due to pilfering'.

"Could You Turn Down The Noise Please"

We liked Munich. We'd played there a lot and is commonly remembered by the Berts for one of their most remarkable feats of endurance, the 21-hour run. Munich had been the last date on a European tour and we wanted to get back home as soon as possible. We finished playing, dived into the van and began driving across Germany. We didn't stop until we got on the ferry in Ostend at dawn. Relays of Berts took turns driving the van, until we managed to get back to Manchester after a hectic 21 hours and 800 miles. We had a night's sleep, grabbed a change of clothing, some new books, and went off to the next gig.

In 1979 we were booked to perform *Sleak* at the Munich International Festival of Drama, organised by Peter Brook and this time, our spell in Munich wasn't so frantic. We played for a week in a field full of tents next to another field where they held the Beer Festival which was running concurrently to the drama festival. We'd no sooner started our performance when a flurry of organisers came rushing into our tent and began gesticulating at the roadies. Doug came over to me at the side of the stage and said, "The theatre company in the next tent have asked us to turn down the music." He was laughing as he said it.

"Who are they?" I asked him.

"The Italian Theatre of The Deaf," he exploded in hysterics.

Now, in the overall scheme of things, while the Berts were a band, we weren't that loud, not as loud as some of the bands we'd played with. And to be asked to turn down the volume was a new and novel experience - certainly we'd never been asked to turn the volume down by a bunch of deaf people before. Andrew went off to find out why.

When he came back he explained that it was the vibrations that were bothering them. Not bad vibes man, but the vibes from Tony's bass.

Elk-a-Hole-Lot-of-Trouble in Finland

How can I begin to describe how Finland was to us in the early 1980s? A lot of pollution has flowed under the bridge since then and I'm sure things have changed a lot, but back then I swear to you, it was the most appalling, Godawfull place that we ever had to perform in.

At our first gig there we arrived, did our soundcheck and then, as was customary, looked around for the bar. I couldn't quite see one, but noticed a huddle of people standing by a hole in the wall with a serving hatch. Correctly deducing that it was where you got drinks from I pottered over thinking to get the first round in. A rather pleasant young woman asked me what I'd like –

"Eight bottles of beer please," I ordered.

"I'm sorry. You can only have one," she replied.

Cursing my lack of Finnish, and assuming I hadn't made myself clear, I repeated the order, only slower and slightly louder … "Eight - bottles - of - beer - pleeeeeease …"

P Simon, Tony and Bruce lift the roof off with their syncopated riffs

She repeated her refusal. I began to take it personally. I gestured round at the band who were sat on the stage looking thirsty.

"You are only allowed to buy one bottle at a time," she told me. "It is the law," she added with a sense of finality that suggested arguing with her would be futile.

I went back to the ensemble clutching my precious bottle.

"You'll have to get your own." I told them.

"You tight bastard," Captain Mog remonstrated with me. "No. No." I told him, "it's the law."

Things got worse that night when we were just about to go on stage and set off carrying bottles of beer. The promoter rushed up and tried to take the off us. "You cannot drink on stage!" he shouted.

"Don't tell us," we snarled, "It's the law."

One musician we knew, used to keep a bottle of spirits in his pocked and a length of rubber tube that went from the bottle, up inside his jacket and was sewn inside his collar; whenever he wanted a drink he'd just suck on the tube. Our solution was simpler ... our sound engineer Glynn emptied out a carton of orange juice and re-filled it with one of our eight bottles of duty-free pure vodka. We shared that carton on stage that night of what turned out to be a not altogether professional set from 'England's funniest Rock men.'

There weren't a lot of laughs either in Lapland where we played a midsummer open-air festival. Set amidst mountains and lakes, the festival site was probably quite nice if you were into scenery. It was only just getting dark when we went on stage at about midnight and the stagelights came on as the night was closing in during our set. To add to our misery, the lights attracted thousands and thousands of flying things. We couldn't see the audience throught the fog of mosquitos. Everytime I took a breath to sing I'd take in a mouthful of bugs ... and not a beer to wash them down with!

And so our stay in Finland dragged on. Alcohol was incredibly hard to come by anywhere - you could only order it in a restaurant with a meal and off licences were open only for a half day a week. So we noticed that when the Finns did get hold of drink they tended to neck it as quickly as possible. And not just beer – they'd drink anything – spirits, reindeer piss, eau de cologne, anti-freeze. It accounted for the unusual sight of business men lying paralytic in the street by mid-day. And weed? Forget it! Our promoter got quite excited when we talked about it and said he remembered somebody having some once ... we remember being glad to get back to Manchester.

Drinking The Penguin Dry

We were offered the chance of a week-long residency in Tel Aviv and we took it because we wanted to see what was going down in Israel. It was highly unlikely that the UN would ever invite me to go on a fact-finding tour, so an all-expenses paid trip was quite attractive. When we arrived at Ben Gurion Airport we couldn't believe how quickly we were whisked through customs and immigration. It turned out that our promoter, a tanned Sabra (Israeli born) chap, called Ari, was an ex drugs squad detective. His girlfriend had given him a tab of acid one day, and after he told her that he liked it, she told him to stop busting people then. So he left the police and ended up promoting Rock gigs in Tel Aviv. Everywhere we went with him people shouted out greetings. He was a very popular man.

Ari drove us to the Tel Aviv Hilton and after booking us unto our rooms handed each one of us a huge lump of Lebanese Red.

"Enjoy your stay," he said with a wicked grin as he shot off to do whatever else it was that he did.

That night we took ourselves off to the gig, the Penguin Club, a kind of Punk palace near the sea front in Jaffa. It was a peculiar place to come across in the Middle East. Mog and I went to the bar and ordered a round of drinks.

"Are you next week's band?" the barmaid asked as we reached for our shekels.

"Er, yes. Why?" we asked nervously.

"Ari said you're to have all your drinks on the house." She answered.

By the end of the evening we'd drunk the bar dry of Heineken but thankfully, by the time we began our residency, fresh supplies had been hauled in from Cyprus.

The generosity had no bounds ... when we began our residency, an amiable young barman, whose name we never got, so we nick-named him 'Dostoevsky' because he acted like an idiot, arrived in the dressing room with a tray laden with Marguerita cocktails, complete with salted rims.

"Ari says you are to have these," he winked.

Had Ario taken out insurance on us or something, we began to wonder? First it was lumps of dope as big as bars of soap, then it was a free bar tab, now it was killer cocktails.

Blasted out of our skulls, sat in the dressing room before a set, a large rat poked its head out of a hole in the dressing room floor and Jimmy shrieked.

"It's alright," said Mog. "It's on the guestlist."

We could perform drunk, we could perform stoned - we were perfect for the Penguin!

When we came off stage, Dostoevsky was there with another tray of Mexican mayhem ... and so it continued all week, taking its toll on us ...

About four nights in, we were playing merrily away when I suddenly realised I couldn't hear John's saxophone. I noticed everybody looking around and there was John lying flat out on the floor. To hell with it we thought, and we carried on, finished the set and came off stage, leaving him there. Next on was an Israeli band and, being either polite or nervous, they left John where he was. Watching their set from out front, suddenly we could hear John's saxophone. He was still lying down, it was halfway through their set and he was playing our tune from exactly where he'd passed out. He rose like a Phoenix and stood triumphant, if a tad unsteadily, amidst the bewildered Israeli performers before taking a bow and leaving the stage.

That same night, back at the Hilton, as helicopter gun-ships flew overhead, their searchlights sweeping the beach for terrorists, we finally realised that tequila also acted as an hallucinogenic when a man wearing a sombrero and poncho arrived at our door. We were listening carefully to what he was saying, and when he'd left we decided that he'd come to give us an award for our services to the Mexican tequila export industry on behalf of Senor Jose Cuervos himself. I've still got a tape I made of the night before the last gig where we estimated that each member of the band had drunk the equivalent of their own body weight at least three times that week.

We never went back to Israel. It was too dangerous we decided.

Coda

I'm standing in a back alley in Rotterdam. It's four in the morning. I'm with Bruce and we're about to climb the stairs of a cheap boarding house. The alley stinks. I do too because I'm soaking with sweat from the gig we've just played. We have to get up in four hours time and drive three hundred miles to the next gig. I've got just about enough cash to buy a meal if we've got time to stop for one. Bruce puts his arm around my shoulder.

"CP? Didn't I tell you if we stuck together we'd go to the top?"

114 WHEN WE WERE THIN

1976 Quartier Latin, Berlin - Flares alert! Flares alert!

Playing for the Stoned Heads of Europe   115

7

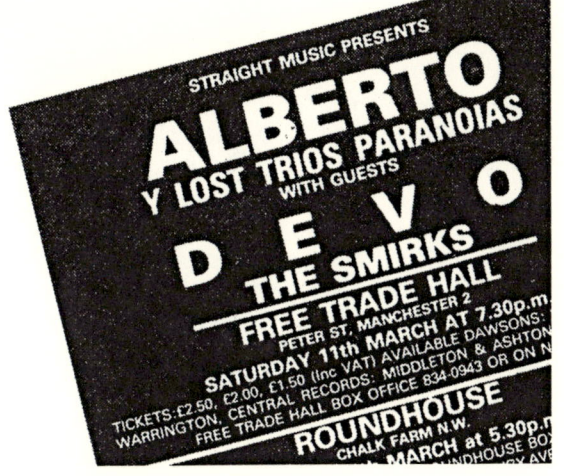

CHAPTER SEVEN
FIXTURES, FORCES AND FRIENDS

STRAIGHT MUSIC PRESENTS

ALBERTO Y LOST TRIOS PARANOIAS
WITH GUESTS
DEVO
THE SMIRKS

FREE TRADE HALL
PETER ST, MANCHESTER 2
SATURDAY 11th MARCH AT 7.30p.m.
TICKETS: £2.50, £2.00, £1.50 (Inc VAT) AVAILABLE DAWSONS:
WARRINGTON, CENTRAL RECORDS: MIDDLETON & ASHTON
FREE TRADE HALL BOX OFFICE 834-0943 OR ON N

ROUNDHOUSE
CHALK FARM N.W.
MARCH at 5.30p.m

I'd known Martin Hannett since 1970. We met at a screening of Andy Warhol's film, *Chelsea Girls* at UMIST in town. All the freaks in Manchester knew one another because there were so few of us. He was studying chemistry as far as I can recall, and it was chemistry that led to his downfall. As we both had the same hair-style (Dylanesque curls) we were obliged to become friends. Even though he was a student Martin's main preoccupations were bass playing, listening to music, and getting high, though not necessarily in that order. After the movie I lent him some Velvet Underground albums and he began to even more seriously investigate the world of aural possibilities.

During my 'break' between Greasy Bear and the Berts, Martin and I did a few gigs together, mainly playing tunes by Arthur Lee and Bonnie Raitt. The most memorable one we did was at a gay club called The Penny Farthing. Les had set it up, I don't know how. We just arrived expecting it to be like any other club. A few minutes after going inside we realised that it was not. To describe it as 'Dante-esque' would be to kind of under-describe the atmosphere of Bacchanalian excess that permeated the premises. Martin was never particularly happy about performing on stage, and when I saw that he'd brought a camp-stool along with him which he set up in front of his amp, I thought he might possibly be taking the concept of being 'laid-back' a tad too far. Then when we started playing and he actually sat on it with his back to the audience, I realised I was right.

Looking back on the gig now, I've been forced to the conclusion that Les had got it together for his own amusement. This was his first ever public gig and he wanted to see what it was like being in front of an audience. He didn't sing, or play, and I don't recall that he even said anything that night. What he did do was freak out the manager of the club, which considering the transvestite barmen, sailors dancing together and unusal events in the gents was no mean feat. Les had arrived just after us and he was carrying a large suitcase. He wouldn't tell any of us what was in it, just kept saying it was for 'the lead breaks, man'.

All was revealed when, in the middle of Love's *Ride That Vibration (Like A Six Foot Wave)*, he came charging on stage with a huge tree-felling axe which he started swinging round his head and 'playing' behind his back like Jimi Hendrix. To us, the joke was immediately obvious – he was playing his 'axe', literally. To the manager, he was a maniac who was directly threatening the safety of his customers.

Shortly afterwards several large bouncers came on stage and ushered Les off. A few minutes after that, Les came rushing back on and started doing it again. The next few numbers were like something out of the Keystone Cops as bouncers and Les came and went, first in one direction, then in another. Finally the manager pulled the plug in the middle of our version of *Singing Cowboy*, and we all went home.

Possibly as a result of this, Martin played live gigs less often. Certainly, he got more involved in the musician's co-operative, Music Force, taking on a variety of roles ranging from agent to organiser, being in charge of the equipment. Practically and obsessively, his growing interest in woofers, tweeters, speakers and such-like would guide the direction he'd take for the rest of his life.

The Human Sampler And Other Friends

"Good evening and welcome to Granada Reports." The face on the screen, introducing the local TV news and weather came as a bit of a shock. Although wearing the obligatory 'talking head' suit and (very wide) tie, the presenter actually looked like one of us. He was in his early twenties and had shoulder length hair. His eyes too, had the look of a man who was no stranger to the works of Aldous Huxley and Timothy Leary. His name was Tony Wilson.

From 1973 onwards, whenever I was at home in Manchester, I'd see Tony Wilson on the telly. More often than not he was out on location somewhere, delivering some absurd report about hang-gliding in Derbyshire, or the biggest cabbage ever grown in Runcorn, but throughout it all he always appeared to be an affable freak who'd landed on his feet and got a job on the idiot box. He also gave the impression that he knew it was all a joke.

Which is how come, when we became friends and I would go round with him to various places, I was amazed and horrified by the level of animosity and hatred that people generated against him. There often seems to be some inbuilt negativity gene in the Northern psyche, that drives folk to pick on those that have somehow 'made it'.

Pete Shelley told me once about going into a pub for a quiet drink. He'd no sooner sat down than a bloke at the bar kept looking at him and nodding his head up and down. Pete nodded back and the guy came over.

P 1975 - Granada Reports

"It's you, you, innit? That bloke in that group. Off the telly?" the man went on, grinning all over his face.

"Yes, that's right," Pete replied, quite proud at being recognised. "Buzzcocks."

"Buzzcocks, right! Do you mind if I fetch me girlfriend over?" he asked Pete.

"No. That's fine." Pete told him. The man went off and returned a moment later with his paramour, who was also grinning and nodding her head up and down. . Assuming they wanted an autograph, Pete reached into his jacket for a pen.

"I just wanted to tell you," the man said, "I think you're shit!" And they walked off.

Wilson used to get that all the time, but without the preliminary niceties. If you're in the public gaze all the time I guess you get used to it, but I never saw the same kind of hatred levelled at anybody else. Mind you, most 'TV celebrities' (famous for being famous) don't tend to go out much, preferring staged managed events when they do. Tony, looked upon himself as simply an ordinary punter and, sharing all the same interests as any other normal person of his age, never hid himself away. Nor, when he did go to public events, did he go as a celebrity ... once an anarchist, always an anarchist. He'd graduated from Cambridge where one of his closest friends was the man who went on to become the editor of Fortean Times, Paul Sieveking. Sieveking's father had been best mates with Aleister Crowley, the 'Great Beast 666', magickian and mystic. Once Tony was helping Paul move one of his father's old pieces of furniture and a secret drawer came open. In it was a note from Crowley. It read "Help me!"

It's All In The Jeans

Another Granada employee who used to knock about with us was Geoff Hughes, who was playing Eddie Yates in *Coronation Street* at the time. We'd often go along together to shows at the Apollo, or the Free Trade Hall, as well as smaller gigs at Irish pubs in Rusholme and Longsight, because we shared a common cause – a desperate search for different music. All three of us were fed up with the fodder on offer. Tony's predilection was for American performers like Neil Young and Tom Waits. In fact, his preoccupation with Neil Young went so far as getting his girlfriend at the time to sew dozens of patches on his jeans so that he looked like the back cover of Young's *After The Goldrush* album. Geoff's taste was for Irish Traditional music, and Country. All we knew for sure was, we didn't like The Eagles or Kiss.

Tony started fronting a regular weekly show on Granada called *What's On* and he was able, every now and again, to present some of the more non-mainstream acts that he liked, including the Berts amongst others. A couple of these appearances stick in the mind, one was Christmas 1976 when we sang an a cappella version of *Adeste Fidelis*, dressed as choir boys. A caption underneath exhorted the viewing public to "Never mind the cassocks". Also on the bill was an up and coming magician called Paul Daniels. Backstage he showed us some very interesting tricks you could

GM 1976 Heil Gittler - Cover shot for New Manchester Review

do with a Rizla packet and its contents. Another time, I appeared on my own in a rowing boat that studio staff shook from side to side. I don't know why, I was just there. Debbie Harry who was also on the show that evening said she found it "very disturbing".

Eventually somebody high up in Granada gave Tony what he'd been dreaming of since he started work there – the chance to do a Rock show. It was called *So It Goes* and was fronted by Clive James. When the executives saw the pilot they realised they weren't going to get an alternative to *Top of the Pops*, but they let it go ahead anyway. Quoting from Mick Middles' *From Joy Division To New Order The Factory Story*, Wilson regarded "90% of the music featured ... as total shit" because of the bands he was forced to showcase. The series was recorded just as the Sex Pistols and Punk were emerging on the scene; of course the second series would be a different story. However, I've got very fond memories of the early days, including an afternoon spent drinking with an acerbic Tom Waits, who talked about cars and Kerouac and how you couldn't get decent whisky in this "damn country" and why did everybody "talk so goddam funny?" He then went back into the studio and delivered a blistering version of *Waltzing Matilda*. And of course the last show of that first series on 4 September 1976 set the scene for those to follow - Wilson, almost by threatening to resign if he didn't get his own way, booked the Sex Pistols to appear on it. It was their first TV appearance, not, as most people think, Bill Grundy's London-only *Today* show in December of that year. And they were dynamite.

Tony stuck his neck out so far for Punk it's a wonder he didn't get his throat cut. One day he showed me the hate mail he was receiving. After having had Buzzcocks on *What's On*, one irate member of the public had written a letter about how he had spent years learning the guitar and now Wilson was putting these talentless geeks on TV, instead of him! This was representative of the music world's great deal of animosity against the newly emerging Punk scene, not just in Manchester, but all over the country.

Meanwhile, the Berts were watching from the sidelines, as it were, before becoming directly involved in the whole thing - after all, we shared the same building in London as Stiff Records ...

If It Ain't Stiff It Ain't Worth A Fuck!

By 1976 we were beginning to earn a living. We were slowly moving our way up the second division and there were plenty of tours lined up, but at Berts London HQ in Bayswater, things were changing. Blackhill moved permanently upstairs into what had been Marc Bolan's flat when he was with Blackhill, and the groundfloor and basement was suddenly occupied by the newly formed Stiff Records. Stiff was founded by Jake Rivera, former manager of our old chums Chilli Willie and The Red Hot Peppers, and Dave Robinson, who'd managed Brinsley Schwartz, and established London's Hope and Anchor pub as a premier venue for bands like Kilburn and The High Roads and Doctor Feelgood. Both of them felt the time was ripe for an independent UK label that reflected the new music that was developing.

If our neighbours in Alexander Street had thought the likes of us, and Kevin Ayer's Whole World (the sight of lead guitarist Ollie Halsall in his bumble bee suit, complete with wings must have seemed a bit odd), what moved in next door then must have been terrifying. First off was The Damned.

They'd only been going for a couple of weeks when Jake signed them, and it was only a couple of weeks after that when Stiff put out Britain's first Punk single *New Rose*, beating Malcolm McLaren and the Pistols by a mile.

Dave Vanium, The Damned's singer was okay. Anybody who dressed like Bela Lugosi as Dracula in the middle of one of the hottest summers on record was fine by us. Likewise Bryan James, who always seemed as if he was dressed up waiting for a call to join the Rolling Stones. Captain Sensible, on the other hand, well. He used to hang around backstage at the Greyhound in Croydon, so we were used to him. The drummer, Rat

GM Bruce and Jack's wedding day. John Dowie behind CP

Scabies, was a little twerp. His idea of fun was to squirt lighter fluid on people then set fire to them When he pissed on the seats in the back of our VW micro-bus, "for a laugh, innit", the Berts' enforcer, Tony Bowers, knocked him out and shoved him in a dustbin outside the office.

Jake was always asking me if we wanted to make a single that would be so pornographic it would be immediately banned everywhere and thusly become a big hit. We'd already discovered that being banned didn't actually amount to a hill of beans, so, for the moment, we gave that one a miss. We all got off on their idea of slogans though – 'In 78, everybody born in 45 will be 33' was a good one, as was – 'Back to mono!' I gave them 'If it ain't Stiff it ain't worth a fuck' and I believe, 'Fuck art, let's dance!' came from us as well.

It was always fun round at Stiff. One day, Nick Lowe and Jake shoved me inside a cab and we went off to meet one of their new signings. Nick was producing his first album in the little converted garage studio that they used. He was called Declan, but was to shortly be re-christened, Elvis Costello. I sat in the control room and watched Nick do his magic, not that Declan/Elvis needed much help. He was laying down vocal tracks. Afterwards we all climbed in another cab and set off for the Marquee where we planned to meet Larry Wallace and refresh ourselves with a few libations. On the way a pigeon flew towards the taxi. Declan/Elvis dived down in his seat and put his hands over his head.

"Sorry," he said. "I've got this thing about birds. I can't stand them."

So there you go. Even a towering colossus of the Pop universe like Elvis Costello proves that he is just as human as the rest of us.

In the bar at the Marquee we met Larry, and Sex Pistols' Steve Jones and Glen Matlock. Everything was going smoothly until Lemmy and some Hells Angels came in. As we were talking I could hear one of the Angels say to Lemmy, "And I bet you ten quid I can do it, man!"
"Bollocks" said Lemmy. "Prove it!"

At this, the Angel turned round and delivered a pile-driving punch into the head of a poor unsuspecting punter, who immediately fell unconscious to the floor. We all watched in astonishment as Lemmy and the Angel stood over the guy and counted how long he remained on the floor. After about ten seconds Lemmy said, "Yeah, but you cheated, man. He wasn't expecting it."

Too right he wasn't and neither were we. We made our excuses and left.

Food

Shortly after that I was back in their studio. Jake had phoned me in Manchester and offered to pay for me to come to London and do a vocal for a track called *Food* that Nick, Dave Edmunds and Larry Wallace had recorded under the group name The Takeaways. They sent me a demo tape and I made arrangements for a long stay. Who knew how long something like this would take ...

As it turned out, three takes. Once as a run through, once in the style of Bob Dylan, and once à la Bryan Ferry. Jake and Nick were immediately sold on the Dylan version. I picked up my cash and off we went for a night on the town. The song finally came out on a compilation album called *A Bunch of Stiffs*, and also as a single in France where I'm told it did reasonable business. On the album the vocalist was un-named "due to contractual commitment with major American company" and it remained a mystery for years. There was a lot of conjecture over whose vocal it was, but the truth was finally revealed in 2006 in Henrik Bech Poulsen's *77 The Year of Punk & New Wave*. Now you know.

The Terrible Twins Dine Out

One morning I was passing Jake on the stairs when he stopped and looked at me quite intently for a moment or two.

"'Ere. You could pass for Elvis (as Declan was now known). Do you fancy earning twenty quid this afternoon?" he asked me.

As I wasn't due on stage until that night, I agreed and asked him what he had in mind.

Jake explained that Island Records (who distributed Stiff in the UK) were holding a big meeting that afternoon with all their reps from around the country. They really liked *My Aim Is True* (Elvis' first album) and he'd told them that Elvis would be there and jolly them all up at the sales push.

"But?" I said.

"He doesn't want to go because it'll be so fucking boring... Twenty quid CP. Think of the money, my son. All you have to do is stand there."

GM CP or Elvis? You decide

It was not only an interesting proposition, but a lucrative one. I readily agreed. I did look like Elvis. We were both the same height, I wore a pair of Buddy Holly glasses and we virtually had the same haircut. I too wore second hand 1960s suits.

"Yeah, alright"

That afternoon I arrived in a taxi at Island Records HQ, and I was ushered, with much ceremony, into the board room where a group of eager young sales reps enthusiastically greeted me. I sat at the head of the table signing autographs while tracks off *My Aim Is True* were played in the background. I was nearly doubling up with laughter and could hardly speak, managing to say nothing more to the assembled throng than - "Let's get out there and shift those units!"

One sales rep approached me and said how, after hearing the album, "I'd expected you to be more serious but you seem such a happy guy." He'll know now how twenty quid can put a smile on the dial.

Another time I also got a really good lunch off Island via Jake. As I approached the office one morning, what looked like a fleet of taxis were pulling up outside. "Quick! Jump in CP!" shouted Jake. Ever ready for an adventure I did as I was bid and a short while later found myself with a dozen or so Stiffettes entering a fairly chichi Italian restaurant in Mayfair. A bevy of disgruntled waiters guided us to a quieter area of the premises, pushing tables together and grumbling about how we should have booked ahead for a party this large.

I found myself sat next to Wreckless Eric, who was acting like a kid at his birthday party he was that happy. I asked him what was going on and found out how Island Records had agreed to some big deal with Jake and they said they'd take him out to lunch to sign the contract and celebrate. Jake had asked if he could bring along a couple of people, and they had agreed. Wreckless was telling me this as he was ordering four large brandies for himself as an aperitif. At the head of the table sat a very satisfied looking Jake and two rather nervous-looking record label executives watching as more people sat down - there must have been about twenty of us.

"Order anything you want kids!" shouted Jake. "It's all on expenses!"

The two execs looked at each other and grinned feebly.

"Waiter" called Jake. "What's the most expensive wine on the menu?"

The Maitre D' pointed haughtily at something on the wine list.

"One each then, for everybody," Jake ordered.

About half way through the meal, Wreckless discovered that he could manoeuvre his table by shunting it with his legs. With a roar of excitement he set off round the restaurant beeping madly and shouting, "Look at me! I can drive my table!"

He hadn't noticed that his tablecloth was tucked under the leg of the table next to him and within seconds his had slid off sending his cutlery and plates smashing to the ground. Ignoring the clatter, he carried on his journey around the room. As a waiter appeared to pick up the shattered pieces I took the opportunity to order more brandy.

Exit Music Force Enter Rabid Records

Tosh Ryan and Martin Hannett were preparing to move on from Music Force, which by 1977 was dying a natural death anyway. In order to supplement his meagre earnings with the Albertos, Bruce had gone into fly-posting. If you wanted a fly posting anywhere in England he was the man to see. No – obviously, I mean, fly-posting posters for concerts. As the Berts became more successful he passed on the rights to Tosh, who became known around the country as 'Superfly'. Before Music Force totally disappeared, its highly moralistic tendencies in shreds, Martin had

JH (L-R) Martin Hannett (standing!), Paul Burgess, Mike King

managed to fulfil one of his dreams and produce a recording. Perhaps not quite the act that he wanted to produce, which basically would have been a band, it was for a Socialist theatre company called Belt and Braces. But it got him into a studio and once he was inside he knew that it was all he ever wanted to do.

The next time he got behind a mixing desk it was for a Hi-Life group from Nigeria who'd approached Music Force about independently producing their own album to sell at gigs. Martin got the job done and he used this second chance to find out about more than just studio techniques. I remember talking to him about how you got records pressed up and labels made and so forth. He was pretty excited and when Howard

Devoto came to see him about putting the Sex Pistols on at the Lesser Free Trade Hall, Martin watched Howard and Pete Shelley's progress with great interest. So did Tony Wilson, who'd been sent a demo tape of the Pistols by Howard, and of course all of them were there at the Pistols' first gig in Manchester, along with about thirty other people. It wouldn't be too far fetched a claim to say that those thirty people went on to form the backbone of the Manchester musical revival that eventually led to 'Madchester' and all that that entails. However, that's another story.

Through his fly-posting business, Tosh was approached by a young band straight out of Wythenshawe, South Manchester's working-class ghetto, Slaughter and The Dogs. Part post Glam Rock, part anger, they wanted to make a single. Martin suggested that they put it out on their own label. He was also telling Howard Devoto and Buzzcocks the same thing.

Martin and Tosh decided to go for broke, left Music Force and bought a run-down shop in Withington and, using fly-posting money for their backing, formed Rabid Records. Rabid's first release was Slaughter and The Dogs *Cranked Up Really High*. Martin, acting as an independent producer, also went into the studio with Buzzcocks and together they made *Spiral Scratch*, which the band put out on their own label, New Hormones. Suddenly, Manchester was a happening.

New Kids On The Block

I was touring in Europe when the Sex Pistols played in 1976. When we came back it was all Tony Wilson could talk about. To most of the musicians in Manchester it was a joke. These were people who'd spent years perfecting their dole technique in order to enable them to avoid having to do unnecessary things like working, while they concentrated on much more important things such as joint rolling, or reading NME. And now all these kids were appearing as if out of nowhere and rejecting all the things that they held dear like long hair and even longer guitar solos, concept albums and flared trousers. That's what hit the old guard worse – the thought that they might be unhip, uncool, out of touch – in plain language, getting old.

All the tired clichés came running out. Punks can't play, can't sing, they're just a fad, a flash in the pan. Even the rusty old canard, stop me if you've heard it before, Johnny Rotten took a dump on stage and then eat it!? Well, I had heard it before. In the 1960s they'd said the same thing about Frank Zappa. I think people had even said it about us! Maybe it was that or that we were shit on stage, I don't know, I can't quite recall.

Another thing that disturbed the peace and tranquillity of the Manchester music scene was the Punk's apparent determination to play on stage. Now that didn't bother the Albertos because stage work was our bread and butter, but for a significant amount of the musos I knew, playing live was anathema attack. Playing live went totally against the grain, it was, well, undignified. Hadn't 'serious' musicians spent years fighting against that sort of thing? You were supposed to form your group, then disappear inside a studio for six months and then emerge with an album which you sold to a major record label who gave you a gigantic advance. In time, you might deign to appear at a festival or undertake a concert tour of large venues in order to promote said album, but even that was perhaps pushing it a bit too far. Pub Rock was tolerated because it paid homage to an earlier, more innocent time, but bands like the Feelgoods and the Kilburns were more of a joke, weren't they?

It slowly began to dawn on the 'serious' types that something was happening and it wasn't going to go away. The Punks were propagating their own scene, and it was attracting audiences. In dismal beer halls like Rafters and disused cinemas like the Electric Circus, a new crowd was gathering. Hair began to be cut, trousers modified, a more working class pose adopted.

In Dem Old Cotton Lane Back Home!

The Rabid offices in Cotton Lane became a kind of unofficial HQ for the newly emerging movement. Situated in an old shop at the end a row of Victorian cottages, you could hardly move for piles of posters waiting to be stuck up, amplifiers, boxes of singles and a huge desk behind which either Martin or Tosh would be sat using the phone. I used to like going down there and hanging round.

One day Martin asked me if I wanted to go and see Warsaw with him that night. He and Tosh were thinking about putting them on Rabid.

"I'm fucking not!" shouted Tosh. "Bunch of Nazi bastards! I'm having nothing to do with them!"

Travelling in Martin's battered Volvo was always an interesting experience because you only had to sit inside it to be stoned. It reeked of dope and the ashtrays were overflowing with roaches. Torn up Rizla packets and empty Benson and Hedges packs littered the dashboard, competing for space with crushed Pepsi cans and hi-fi magazines. In a way the décor reflected the inside of Martin's head, dozens of different ideas jumbled together looking for a way out

We parked up and went inside Salford Technical College and for the first time I saw what was to become Joy Division. They were dark and gloomy, but I didn't quite get the 'Nazi' angle that Tosh had been raging about. On the way home Martin said, "They're the future! That's where it's going, man!" I threw out the phrase 'Thin young men with minds as narrow as their ties', but Martin just laughed. Later, I tried out 'Manchester Miserablists' on him, but it was too late by then, their futures were intermingled and Destiny could not be denied.

P 1979 - Tosh at Rabid (Cotton Lane)

Fac2 - A Factory Sample

Martin and Tosh carried on putting out an eccentric mixture of 'product' on Rabid – John Cooper Clark's *Psycle Sluts*, where the Salford

Bard was backed by Martin, Steve Hopkins (from 1960s Manchester psychedelic band Gemini Zent), and soon to be an Alberto, John Scott. These musicians, along with several others, and always supervised by Martin, would become the Rabid house-band – Martin's equivalent of Phil Spector's 'The Wrecking Crew', or more properly, given Martin's penchant for narcotics, 'The Wrecked Crew'. Graham Fellowe's alter ego, Jilted John also emerged on Rabid and was quickly leased to EMI, and became a top ten hit. Ed Banger and The Nosebleeds with the brilliantly violent *Aint Bin To No Music School* and football anthem, *Kinnel Tommy!* were also Rabid releases ...

Meanwhile during summer 1977, Tony Wilson and his mate Alan Erasmus had been sitting around Rabid watching how things were done and on the cusp of 1978 after a meeting in Liverpool with Roger Eagle and a small amount of acid, Tony decided to set up a label as well. Alan saw a sign on a wall 'Factory Clearance' and Manchester's second independent record label, Factory was born.

I decided it was time I got a slice of all this production action and zoomed in heavily for the inclusion of a side by the lovably eccentric Brummie, John Dowie. He'd just been dumped by his label Virgin after a certain amount of controversy had been generated by a track called *I Hate The Dutch* – "The Dutch are mad, they ride around on bikes" is a taster enough. Tony Wilson agreed that Dowie should be on Factory. The puzzled comic was bundled into a van along with Tony Bowers, Simon Tommy White, Bruce Mitchell and me and poured into Cargo Studios, Rochdale, home of the legendary Tractor Records, where we cut four tracks. And do you want to know why the result, Fac2, a Factory Sampler, is worth so much money? Forget the embryonic Durutti Column, the quirky charm of Joy Division, or the clapped out synth sound of Orchestral Manoeuvres In The Dark, Dowie is the man who gives it its cutting edge brilliance, aided in no small way by my production techniques that involved making sure everybody in the studio had taken large enough amounts of amphetamine in order to sound as much as possible like the early Velvet Underground.

In the Bunker with Buzzcock

The first time I met Buzzcocks they were walking down some stairs in an office block on Peter Street in town. Pete Shelley had a ghetto blaster and it was playing Captain Beefheart's *Lick My Decals Off, Baby*. I was very impressed and said as much to their manager Richard Boon. We agreed there and then to become friends for life, which we've been. Even when year later I stole The Smiths' gold record for their first album off the wall of Rough Trade and sent in a Polaroid photo of a hand holding a gun to it and a ransom demand for a cup of sugar 'or the gold record gets it', he forgave me and made sure I was allowed back in Rough Trade when Geoff Travis wasn't around.

Back in those early days of our friendship, it seemed like a good idea to get Pete Shelley to produce some tunes we had lying around and so the Berts and Pete found ourselves in the studio together. It was about the time that electronic drum sounds were emerging, and Pete demonstrated that you didn't need expensive equipment to get that peculiar 'whoomph' sound. You simply had to place a pillow over somebody's mouth and punch them in the stomach. On another occasion I managed to persuade him to go into the studio with me and we cut a disco version of *Shot By Both Sides*, that came out on New Hormones in 1981 and is now available on the Overground Records' Albertos compilation CD *Radio Sweat*.

THE ALBERTOS pretend that they're just kidding around with typical Mancunian deadpan wackiness and not really commenting on PETE SHELLY's production techniques. Pic: KEVIN CUMMINS.

Enter Kick-Boy Face

As Factory got more successful, Tony started taking himself more seriously. Once upon a time we used to sally forth, senses heightened with liberal doses of hallucinogens and make merry with the night, whereas nowadays, as he climbed up the social and artistic ladder, he got harder to approach. One night I was watching his latest signing, A Certain Ratio, and I told him I didn't like them. He started screaming at me and quoting lines from Dylan's *Times They Are A Changin'*. Matters weren't helped by the fact that one of the Albertos was having an affair with his first wife, Lindsay.

When Tony, Rob Gretton and Alan Erasmus, announced the opening of the Haçienda, Martin, who was the fourth director of Factory, wanted nothing to do with it. He thought the idea was crazy and that they should be putting their money into a studio. I was friends with both Tony and Martin and it was tough for me juggling over the pros and cons of who should be coming round for dinner and suchlike. Tony was committed and focused on the club and though it was uncomfortable for me, the gulf between us all was widening and Martin began to nurse a grudge that would never really go away.

One afternoon Rob Gretton asked me if one of their employees from the Haçienda could stay with me for a little while. I said sure and the next thing was a Frenchman arrived on my doorstep. He was called Claude Bessey and he was to spend the next three years living half the week in my house and the other half back in London with his partner, Philly.

Claude had left France in April 1968 because "Nothing ever happened there, it was so fucking boring!" and he'd gone to India where he lived for the next few years operating a wonderful scam whereby he'd arrange for young American girls to be repatriated by their Embassy. Repatriation was the usual outcome when you had run out of money and so, upon their arrival back home the American Customs officials never bothered to look into the backpacks they'd travelled back with. Exploiting this situation, Claude would fill them with hash and with the resulting profits from this unique brand of smuggling he was able, eventually, to emigrate to the States. He took to American ways with great gusto, learning English from the TV – when leaving a room he'd say, "Hey, don't go away. I'll be back right after this break!" – and he settled there for a while.

P Claude Bessey - aka Kick-boy Face

In LA, Claude got a couple of acting jobs - would you believe he played the part of 'Frenchy' in *The Hardy Boys* TV series? He hung out in some of the lowest dives in Mexico and was rapidly becoming very bored yet again when Punk came along and saved his life. Diving headfirst into an amphetamine-crazed lifestyle, Claude started up LA's first Punk fanzine, *Slash*, which was to lead to the setting up of Slash Records. He wrote for Slash under the name of 'Kick-Boy Face', and he had a Punk band called Catholic Discipline, who were featured in Penelope Spheeris' documentary of the LA Punk scene, *The Decline Of Western Civilisation*.

Then LA got too hot for him and he and Philly moved to England. Wilson had offered him a job as video jockey at the Haçienda.

Claude was a manic, speed-driven entity who I immediately took to. I asked him why he'd sought me out – "They told me you were a crazy motherfucker!" Claude always spoke in exclamation marks. "What's wrong with this town anyway?! Why are they so pissed off with my videos?!"

GM John Scott jammin' with John Cooper Clarke

Claude's videos were not your usual run-of-the-mill, let's-go-down-to-the-disco-and-watch-a-Pop-group thing. They were a frantic, blurring mélange of Nazi rallies, Kung-Fu fighting, psychedelic lightshows and fragments of surreal news clips. They were a breathtaking, mind-boggling, brain-numbing blur of shattered fragments of the 20th Century set to a soundtrack that no-one but Claude could hear. Autopsies vied with Donald Duck for screen space. Hitler segued into Salvador Dali holding a mass for the souls of the damned in outer space. There were probably five of us in the world who knew what he was on about, certainly not the average club goer in Manchester. But Tony kept him on.

Christmas Day 1982 and Tony threw a party at his house in a fashionable part of south Manchester. Guests were forced to sit through a Franco Zeffirelli directed video of the Pope holding a High Mass at St Peter's in Rome. So we were watching it when Claude, holding back a grin whispered, "You know we call him the human sampler?" nodding in Tony's direction ... "All you have to do is have an idea and four minutes later he'll come up with it." I wasn't immediately sure what he meant, but he had my attention anyway.

"It'd be a great idea to make the toilets at the Haçienda mixed," said Claude.

True enough, about fifteen minutes later Tony said – " Wouldn't it be a great idea if the toilets at the club were mixed."

Claude just about broke up with laughter.

Stiff Meets So It Goes

Whenever we had the time and when Roger had booked anybody particularly interesting at Erics, we would make a trip over to Liverpool. So when Tony Wilson had booked Elvis Costello and it was decided to film the gig live at Erics, and with Nick Lowe performing too, we chose to go for what promised to be a memorable evening of music and mayhem.

Roger was in one of his periodic fits of enthusiasm, this time over a 'new' drink that he'd invented.

"It's better than speed, man!" he loudly proclaimed. "Just one of them and you're away!"

He led me over to the bar, ordered two of his 'regulars' and handed me a glass of yellow, thick liquid. I sniffed it apprehensively and took a sip. It seemed vaguely familiar.

"Er, what's in it?" I asked him as Roger gulped his down in one.

"Brandy! You have to have brandy! That's the alchemical base for it. It took me ages to find the right one. Vodka's no good, gin's no good. It has to be brandy!"

I had another sip. "And what else?" I asked him.

"Ah! That's where I hit the nail on the head! What do you add to it? Most people have Coke, but that's not got the same quality of rush about it. I wanted to invent something that picked you up and sent you on your way without braining you!" He enthused, ordering another and grabbing the bottle from the barmaid. He brandished it in my face.

"Advocaat! Dutch Advocaat! Made from eggs, you know!"

I did know, but I didn't have the heart to tell him it was what my mother used to drink every Christmas, Advocaat and brandy. Her and my aunties called them 'snowballs'.

Nick Lowe came on first and did a solo set while cameramen flustered around, hampered by the crowd. Wilson looked on happily as Nick delivered high quality performances accompanied only by his electric guitar. It was a great thing to do at that point in musical history. Being alone on stage, lit by a single spotlight made the audience concentrate even more on his songs, and the more they did that, the more he gave out. I turned to Jake Rivera who was looking relieved rather than happy.

"Lazy bastard couldn't get a band together in time," he hissed.

When Elvis and The Attractions came on Erics went wild. For all the time he'd been living in London, this was still the hometown boy made good as far as the Scousers were concerned. He dive-bombed his way through a thirty minute set made up of tunes from the first album, and left them screaming for more. I was backstage with him and Jake when Tony Wilson and his director came in.

"That was really great. We really enjoyed that." They told him. "But we weren't happy with some of the camera work and wondered if you could do it again?"

Elvis merely looked up. Jake, however, went ballistic.

"Again!? Again!?" He stormed. "Just because your poxy cameras weren't ready! This is a fucking Rock band, not a museum!"

The footage was broadcast as was.

The Dark Lords Close In

Martin came round one night and we sat listening to records. We had an argument about The Violent Femmes. Martin insisted that the bass had been equalised and put through a phaser. I told him it had to be a

Mexican Mariachi acoustic bass. A few weeks later Violent Femmes played at the Haçienda and the bass player had an acoustic Mariachi bass.

I figured he was getting too much involved in the noise of production. He was having late-night assignments on top of the moors with an engineer from an electronics firm over in Yorkshire. It was getting like a spy film. He could visualise sound and I've never met anybody in the whole world who could do that. Maybe it hurt his head? No one else could see it the way he did. He used to give drawings of what he saw to another Martin, Martin Usher. He was an early computer buff and close friend of us both. He could sometimes understand Hannett better than I could, especially when they were talking about studio equipment, but even he couldn't grasp the tonal depth of Martin's vision. Whatever, Martin was getting too involved in trying to prise those sounds from out of his head.

One night Martin came round and we were sat listening to records. He handed me a joint and I felt an explosion of cotton-candy in my insides. The most peaceful feeling enveloped me, like I was being wrapped in warm cotton wool. I became mellow like there hadn't been a word for mellow invented yet, it was so new, so fragrant, so blissful. I began to float off. And then I felt sick, a totally deranged sickness. A nausea so strong that waves of it crashed over me like lumps of shit hitting a flower. I grabbed the arms of the chair retching and gasping for breath. Martin just smiled. I crawled off to the bathroom to be sick.

When I got down, Martin had gone home. I began to understand what he'd just given me. Even though I said nothing, he never tried to give me heroin again.

Afterwords

Not at that point, but later on, I 'lost' touch with Martin. Not because I disagreed with what he was doing to himself, but because I couldn't bear to watch his slow decline into the world of the junky. He ignored everybody's please to stop. I'm no angel myself and I certainly don't want to sound like a hypocrite. A lot of people who get into it, get out of it, and Martin finally did. Unfortunately he'd done a lot of damage to his body through a variety of causes over the years, and in 1991, he died.

Martin and Damson and Les and Jules and Rob and Paul and Ian and Claude and Steve and Ray and Tony and on and on, all have passed on in their different ways. all of them are waiting for us in the ballroom of the

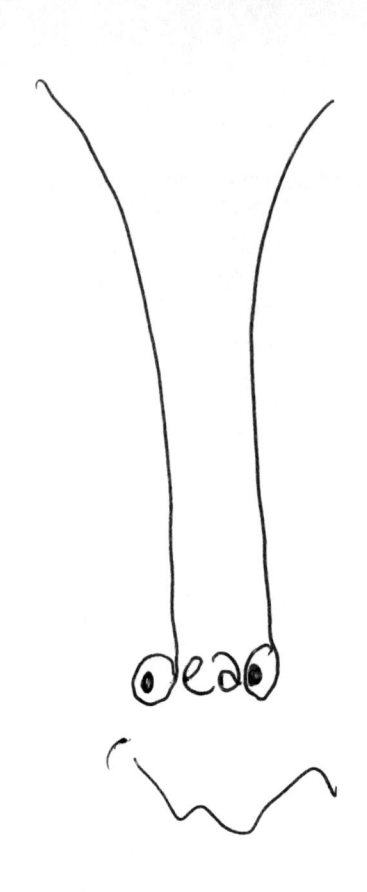

CHAPTER EIGHT

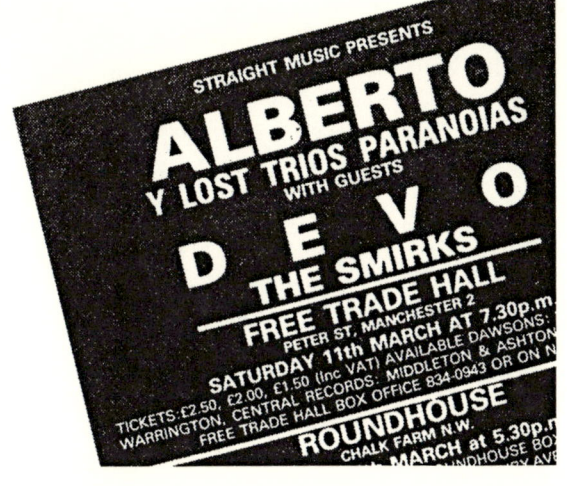

SLEAK: A FUN SHOW ABOUT DEATH

8

STRAIGHT MUSIC PRESENTS

ALBERTO Y LOST TRIOS PARANOIAS
WITH GUESTS
DEVO
THE SMIRKS

FREE TRADE HALL
PETER ST, MANCHESTER 2
SATURDAY 11th MARCH AT 7.30p.m
TICKETS: £2.50, £2.00, £1.50 (inc VAT) AVAILABLE DAWSONS: WARRINGTON, CENTRAL RECORDS: MIDDLETON & ASHTON, FREE TRADE HALL BOX OFFICE 834-0943 OR ON N

ROUNDHOUSE
CHALK FARM N.W.
MARCH at 5.30p.m

A lot of people reckon that roadies are simply 'wannabe' musicians, who, possibly because they haven't got 'what it takes', have shifted sideways along the food chain, in order to remain part of the group. This is not correct. It's true that roadies are of human origin, but there the similarities end. I believe, but have never been able to conclusively prove, that somewhere around the age of ten, or even earlier, 'proto-roadies' are picked up by alien search vessels, carried off to the mothership and taken away to another galaxy for re-grooving.

There, an ancient race of beings coach them in the subtle art of 'roadying' – Lifting big wooden boxes, driving for endless hours without a map on a diet of speed and beer, brainwashed into believing that there is nothing more interesting in the universe than the sex-life of an amplifier, especially in an unholy union with a soldering iron. Moaning and whining are high up there on the alien curriculum of roadyness, along with stating the obvious, "This amp's broken", and outright lying, "I'll have it fixed in three minutes".

When all their programming is completed, successful young roadies are awarded the aliens' highest honour – the multi-purpose, keyring chain of office which is worn round the waist and has on it all those funny little things you get in Christmas crackers, like novelty bottle openers, miniature spanners, allen keys and worn out jokes. All knowledge of their trip across the galaxies is then erased (often taking out other functioning parts of their brains as well) and they're shipped back to earth to await the call.

Starting with Dimitri, his ambulance and PA, the Berts had a variety of roadies who brightened up our otherwise dull and routine lives.

Not quite as good looking as Debbie Harry

We had big strong roadies, Steve Bostock, we had tall roadies, Black Paul Young, we had short roadies, Harry Demac, we had one proper roady, Mike Clement, we had female roadies, Penny and Tessa, we had Scottish roadies, Fraser and Jimmy, we even had very exotic foreign roadies, Dutch Jan (who came back to live in England with us) and Wolfgang from Munich, besides many others from a variety of backgrounds.

Once upon a time we had a roady called Elliot Rashman. He wanted to break into the world of Rock. He'd just graduated from college and was friends with the band. We needed a roady for a European tour and took him on board. Never one to do things by half, Elliot went straight round to 'Roadies R Us' and bought a pair of Oshkosh bibbed overalls, some work boots and his own key ring. He looked just the part. Only trouble was, he hadn't been abducted by aliens. Either that, or something had gone wrong with his programming. He never got past Amsterdam; one ride to Dover and a ferry trip to the Hook of Holland, a quick sprint

BW Berts have ways of making you enjoy the gig

down the autobahn and a set up in the Melkweg and he was all done in. He flew himself home the next day. Still, Elliot's time with the Berts wasn't wasted. He became social secretary of Manchester Polytechnic, and was introduced by Roger Eagle to a young singer called Mick Hucknall. Roger had been doing what he'd done to me in the 1960s – tying him in a chair and making him listen to thousands of records that would point the way to eventual chart success. I guess Roger had more records by the time he got his hands on Mick, because he became Simply Red. Elliot, who became his manager, became simply rich by practising the Andrew King credo of 'dynamic management' – Hire 'em and fire 'em – Keep getting rid of the backing band and stick with the front man.

Like Exotic Animals In An Insane Zoo ...

The closer I lived to these strange creatures, the better I was able to observe their rituals and behaviour. Being essentially an egalitarian outfit, the Berts always regarded roadies as 'co-workers'. I was rudely awakened to the fact that this wasn't necessarily a view shared by them when we were relaxing by the side of a Hilton Hotel swimming pool on one of our later European jaunts.

Pool service had just delivered another round of beers when Dutch Jan spoke up from his reclining position on one of the sun-loungers. The conversation had somehow strayed into politics.

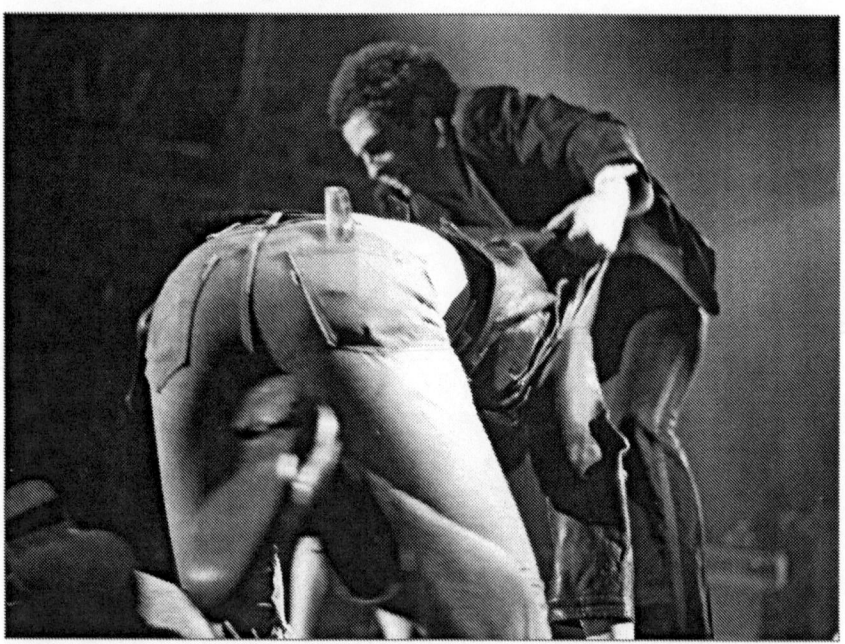

BW Filthy capitalist exploits worker

"Yeah. I'm exploited," said Jan. "Basically I'm one of the proletariat selling the fruit of my labours to you lot – Pass the sandwiches." Hmm ... Jan was six-foot two and ruggedly handsome with shoulder length curly hair. If there'd been a university of handsomeness he would have been the Chancellor for life. The fact that he attracted more women than the Alberto official babe magnet Jimmy Hibbert hadn't gone unnoticed ... We'd have to keep an eye on Jan.

BW 1978 - Manchester Free Trade Hall

We had to keep an eye on all the other roadies too, for a variety of reasons. Scotch Jimmy was given the rather more relaxed job of driving the band's van. We arrived at dawn one morning in Belgium and he cunningly drove off the ferry thus allaying any fears we had as regards his innate sense of direction. These fears however, were to resurface ten minutes later, when, after a quick jaunt around the docks, he drove us straight back on the ferry. Even now, late at night, in a moment of reverie, I can hear the sound of his forehead repeatedly hitting the steering wheel and his tormented voice going – "Bloody foreigners! Bloody foreigners!"

Fraser, his Scottish compatriot, used to amaze us with his seeming ability to exist solely on beer. He assured us that alcohol contained all the proteins and vitamins the human body needed to sustain life at a functioning level. He was saving all the cash he would have spent on unnecessary food for his 'dream studio' back home, and drank only what was his rightful share of our free beer that came with our contract rider. Towards the end of one German tour he was becoming so weak that he could barely lift a bottle to his lips. I remember watching in horror as he lifted a speaker cabinet on to the top of another and it came crashing down on his head. We rushed up and pulled him out from under a tangle of equipment. After checking the speaker first we asked him if he was hurt in any way and as he rubbed the top of his head he replied ruefully, "Only mah dignity, only mah dignity".

Mark Sheppard, who not only roadied for us but also acted in *Sleak* in New York, enquired during an idle moment in the van – "How should

BW The mass ranks of the Funkwaffe

you cook a lobster?" We'd just had a week off and his mum thought she'd send him back to the tender arms of the Berts with a full belly. She'd gone and bought a live lobster. None of his family knew the correct way of cooking one so she'd put some stock, onions and carrots in a casserole dish, plonked the lobster in it and popped it in the oven. After about fifteen minutes the family heard a tapping noise coming from the cooker. It was one of those cookers that had a second door on the inside, made of Pyrex. When they opened the front oven door they were quite surprised to see the lobster, having climbed out of the casserole dish, banging on the glass door with its claws. It was getting hot in there and it wanted out.

"What did you do?" we enquired breathlessly.

"Opened the door," Mark answered...

"And?!"

"Well, we popped it back in the casserole."

"They're Funny Looking Roadies"

As the act got more 'professional' and there were more than enough props, gags and tricks to keep everybody happy, so we began to need a road crew that could do more than drive and lift things. Obviously the most coveted position in the roady hierarchy is that of 'sound-mixer', obvious to most bands that is, and we did have professionals who excelled in that area, Mike Clement and Harry Demac being two that spring to mind. Being concerned with the 'look' of the stage show as well, the Berts took on board two extra members who were more than adequately skilled in specific areas. Both were women – Tessa, who acted as stage manager, and Penny who became our head rigger. She handled the lights and always seemed at her most happy thirty feet up in the air, a joint firmly clamped between her teeth.

They had all the right gear too - the Oshkosh overalls, key rings on chains, etc - and blended in perfectly. Well, almost, that is. Tessa had a lot more strings to her bow than being a stage manager. She was into lots of circus stuff too, fire breathing, tight-rope walking, that kind of thing. She was forever trying out new stunts. Once at Heathrow airport she kept shooting past us in the departure hall. Just gliding by, whooping and hollering. She was riding one of those new fangled skateboard things, and after a bit of badgering let us have a go. We all ended up on the floor after having gone about a millionth of a foot before falling off. She, on the other hand, just kept gliding by. On another occasion I was startled when she went past me about six foot over my head. Yes, it was on a pair of stilts she was practising with. Occasionally she'd incorporate bits of her schtick into the Berts' act, but mainly we just let her set off explosions.

When we were in New York, Union regulations dictated that we had to have an American pyrotechnics roady, so in typical Blackhill fashion Andrew went out and got us a suitably psychotic roady, a Vietnam vet. I think he was the role model for Travis Bickle. Bear in mind that the war had only been over for a couple of years and there were a lot of these guys around. Another close associate of ours over there was an ex-CIA spook called Louis. He always wore a suit and had a shaved head. He was never without his aluminium brief-case, but he'd never let you see what was inside it. Anyway, mysterious as Louis was, he was nowhere compared with the 'Firework Man' - he was very quiet and quite menacing. He'd been an explosives expert in Special Forces and always took great pride in his new-found job in showbiz. After having been in enforced proximity to him over a fairly long period of time however, I could see why the Viet Cong won.

Firework Man wore his badly burn-marked army fatigue jacket all the time though apparently he had a camouflage jacket too but couldn't find it. His face also was covered in burn marks. Throughout the show, pretty well every night, at exactly the wrong point, there'd be a loud bang off stage as Firework Man exploded once more. Once, when there should have been an explosion but never was, he was at the emergency room in hospital instead of at the theatre. We couldn't get rid of him because he was a 'friend' of Louis's. But you could be sat in a bar with him and he'd suddenly explode. Or in an elevator with him and he'd suddenly explode. Being an 'explosives expert' he casually kept his pockets stuffed with chargers and primers and fuses. What he refused resolutely to acknowledge or to take into account at all was the unnatural build up of static electricity in the atmosphere of New York. Normal residents can get a shock just touching a doorknob. Hence the continuing capacity for Firework Man to explode sporadically was simply part of his 'normal' existence. What was worse was that 'Firework Man' had got it into his head that I was some kind of 'buddy' of his, a "crazy fucker" just like him. "You should be honoured," Louis told me, "He killed a lot of gooks."

An Idea Is Born

After the show one night I was stood at the bar of De Lantaaren in Rotterdam with Doug Marnoch. Doug was probably the longest serving Albertos' roady. A very tall ex-policeman with hardly any teeth he fitted in perfectly with our overall view of things. That night, things hadn't gone too well on stage. The PA had broken down for about fifteen minutes at the beginning of the set and I'd berated him from the side of the stage.

"You know what I hate about you lot?" Doug asked me over a Heineken or ten. "I spend three days driving to a gig, four hours setting everything up and then you lot come on stage and ruin it!"
I stood beside him entranced.

"You run about, you knock things over – you sing into the mikes! – And then what?! You bugger off and I have to start all over again!"

Back in England I mulled this little outburst over and got the germ of an idea for a stage-show. I'd also been reading reports in the paper about an American newsreader who'd committed suicide, live on-air. If you combined the two things together within a Rock context then I figured we might have an interesting project.

Playing gigs was becoming a bit too easy. Generally speaking we could guarantee to go down well wherever we played (with the exception of an agricultural college somewhere down South that had refused to pay us because "We didn't like it. We thought you'd play disco music" – At the end of our set the DJ said, "They call themselves the Albertos. I call them shite."). There was an air of change in the wind. Punk was looming over the horizon. Not that we had much to fear from those quarters. The Punks liked us because we hated pretty much the same things they did. But gigging wasn't a challenge any more.

> **Albertos musical**
> ALBERTO Y Lost Trios Paranoias star in a musical play, Razorblades And Roundshot, this month at the Devas Street Theatre in Manchester. Razorblades And Roundshot will run from May 25-28.

Encouraged by Andrew I locked myself away for a while and started writing a comedy script. We booked the Squat, our old 'laboratory', and made plans to open a show, whatever its name or its focus, by Easter 1977. And it came together – characters first. Norman Sleak, the Mandy (mandrax) Freak, would be on the dole and desperately looking for a job. He now had a girlfriend, Sandra, a female plumber, and two mates, Eric and Dave. The four of them would hang out down at the Bondage A Go-Go Club, their local haunt. The show opens with Norman learning that he's got a week to find a job or his dole will be cut off. At the same time, headliners for the night at the Bondage, the Berts are being bawled out by their manager Sammy Sphincter. The band is hopeless, he tells them. If they don't come up with a gimmick quick, they're all washed up. At the Club Norman meets the band's roadies, Jack Plugg and Mike Lead. They tell Norman that life on the road isn't all it's cracked up to be (as in the experiences known to us). Sammy arrives and has a brainwave. He's thought of the very gimmick that will take them to the top – an on-stage suicide. All they need is an idiot who'll take the job. Jack and Mike point out Norman. Sammy moves in like a shark and gets Norman to sign on the dotted line.

The second half of the show is the Albertos' set, throughout which Sammy and the roadies try and help Norman 'accidentally' die. Rather like Wiley Coyote however, all their attempts at helping him on his way to oblivion meet with failure and they're the ones who end up being blown up, electrocuted or otherwise maimed and hurt. During the final number, Norman does accidentally kill himself and a star is (posthumously) born.

That was it. Only it wasn't called *Sleak* at that point. For some obscure reason it went under the name *Razor Blades and Roundshot – A Kind of Musical Play*.

There were a lot of rough edges that needed ironing out. At the first production meeting we had a read through and I asked if everybody was happy with things. Geoff Hughes, who was using his break from Coronation Street to play Norman's mate, Eric, spoke up.

"Er, yeah, There's just one thing," came his unmistakeable Liverpool accent. "This script's shit." And with a flourish he tore it in two and flung it in the air.

"Only joking CP. Only joking!" he said, retrieving the fragments.

Two students, Steve Dixon and Dave Carradine, from the drama department at Manchester University played Jack and Mike, the roadies. Bob Harding played Dave, Norman's other mate, and Julie Williams, a local actress stepped in to play the part of Sandra. In the first half I played myself when the band appeared and in the second part I became Sammy Sphincter, the manager. Jimmy Hibbert took the lead as Norman. Les was too ill to be in the first production.

BW Where Have All The Flowers Gone?

Tickets were printed on P45s and the show's run of four nights sold out almost immediately. Andrew came up from London and I could instinctively sense some dynamic management brewing when he brought along with him a whizz-kid director. This was another drama department graduate, Charlie Hanson, who was then working for the Royal Court Theatre in London. After the final night Andrew announced that Charlie was going to direct the show and it was going to be put on at the Royal Court as part of Prince Charles's Jubilee celebrations.

"So we're all going to London then!" the cast shouted enthusiastically.

"Erm, no. Only the band. We're getting London actors in for the other parts," Andrew told everybody. Geoff nodded sagely. "Charlie will direct the show."

And so it came to pass that we found ourselves rehearsing in Manchester with Arthur Kelly, from TV's *The Chinese Detective*, as Mike, and Gorden Kaye, of *'Ello 'Ello* fame as Jack. Julie Walters played the part of Sandra. The week before opening at the Royal Court we were going to do a 'dry run' at Roger Eagle's club in Liverpool, Eric's.

The new professional cast made a big difference. Gorden in particular was full of gags and ideas for the scenes between the roadies and Sammy. I watched in wonder as their parts grew much larger than originally written. The show now had a new name – *Sleak – The Snuff Rock Musical*, and Les had re-joined the cast as a manic DJ. The rehearsals got tighter and tighter, Charlie teased the best out of all the performers and we prepared to move in on Liverpool the following night.

Then Julie Walters left. We had twenty-four hours to go and she disappeared leaving a message that she had to go back as her boyfriend was jealous. A little while later this was changed to a sick note saying she had 'exhaustion' and couldn't perform. I swore I'd never work with her again, and it's true. To this day I've never worked with her again.

With just twenty four hours notice, Charlie found a replacement for the run at Erics ... Julie Williams stepped back in. *The Liverpool Echo* came down and wanted to interview some of us. One of Roger's mates said, "Why not talk to the girl playing Sandra? She went to school in Liverpool." This was news not only to us, but to her as well. When the interview took place in the dressing room – "Liverpool girl steps in to save play" ran the headline – every time the journalist asked a question, one of Roger's helpers would dive in and give some answer about which school she'd been to and how much she was looking forward to performing in Eric's. It was ludicrous, but it worked.

Ray Lowry's original review for NME

Everything fell into place with the production. Charlie directed a lot of the looseness out of it, the musical numbers were tight and Les, well Les was something else altogether. He'd been working on his part in secret. Because he was so unpredictable and had come into it quite late, there was no way he could have had a role as one of the central characters, but the role he had, that of the Bondage A Go-Go Club's resident DJ, he made uniquely into his own, acting as some kind of manic Greek chorus throughout the proceedings. From the moment that the audience started coming into the venue, Les was on form, looking even more bizarre than he usually did. He stood behind his DJ booth and let rip with a string of gags, ad-libs and raps that never ceased to amaze people. Boxes full

> ALBERTO Y LOST TRIOS PARANOIAS DON'T MISS
> SLEAK! THE RETURN OF SLEAK!
> With Alberto y los. etc. Michael Deeks,
> Judy Lloyd, Arthur Kelly and Gorden Kaye
> at the ROYAL COURT THEATRE, Sloane Square, London W1
> Until 1st October at 8.00 p.m.
> All seats bookable. Box Office: 01-730 1745.

of singles bought from junk shops fed his act and were hurled around, exploded and stamped on. His introductions were ridiculously tasteless, hilarious and mad –

"Here's the Pink Floyd – See Emily Play With Herself."

"This is Bob Marley and The Marley Tiles – Bathroom Inna Babylon"

All of this segued into that 'real rocking foot stamper' Lou Reed's *The Bed*, featuring Les singing along to lines like "This is the room where she slashed her wrists ..."

The week after Liverpool we went to London and met the new Sandra, actress Judy Lloyd. *Sleak* had a week-long run and was immediately booked back by the Royal Court for a season. For some bizarre reason it seemed to hit all the right buttons. The Royal Court is in Sloane Square, at the top of the Kings Road. Outside the whole area was swarming with Punks and tourists looking for Punks. Every Saturday there were running battles between Punks and Teds, the papers loved it and because we were in the middle of it we kept copping the publicity. We soon became the hottest ticket in town.

It felt like everybody wanted to see the show that celebrated death on stage. Celebrities were queuing to come backstage after the show –

Lionel Bart, Julie Christie, Ray Davies, Slaughter and The Dogs! – A never ending stream of people wanted to go for drinks with us in the pub next door. We made the front page of *Time Out*, Jimmy and I did in-depth interviews for newspapers and magazines, ranging from the *Herald Tribune* to *The Times*.

The fake fanzine that we put together for the show, *Kill It* was full of badly- typed and Xeroxed interviews with 'Snuff Rock' stars, and reviews of non-existent groups - It ended up selling 35,000 copies. and years later being quoted in Greil Marcus's *Lipstick Traces*. Hell, if we'd known that killing yourself on stage was going to be that big we would have done it a heck of a lot earlier. Another big spin-off seller was Blackpool rock with the word "Snuff" running through it.

Sleak went on to break all box-office records at the Royal Court, beating even those of the glory days of the 'Angry Young Men' hits of the 1950s and 60s. As the show reached the end of its run, Andrew said that we should transfer somewhere else and carry on milking the gravy train. Off we went to the Roundhouse in Chalk Farm. We were fast becoming the new Rocky Horror Show. Coach loads of Japanese tourists were being shipped in to see the hari kiri Albertos' style. What they must have made of it, who knows. The Pink Floyd's technical crew got involved and soon the place was full of lasers and giant model aircraft on piano wire whizzing around the auditorium. Real Rock stars kept getting killed adding a list of brand new jokes to the script.

One of the reasons behind the show's success was that it pulled in punters who wouldn't normally go to see a play in a theatre. Rock music and thespians usually don't mix well, there's only ever been a handful of crossover hit shows, *Sleak* gave hundreds of young men and women the chance to say to their mates, "Let's go to the theatre tonight." and share in the anarchic zeal that's normally only displayed in the wild or at a zoo.

But playing the same place and the same show night after night began to get boring for most of the Berts. So we stopped the show at the height of its popularity and went back on the road. Andrew tried to persuade me to let the show carry on running with a cast of actors taking over our parts, but I was horrified at the idea of somebody else playing me, and off we trundled, back on the road again. Looking back on it now, it was the most stupid thing I ever did.

Of course, there was always the thought and hope that we could take the show over to America. Almost everyone who'd seen it said it couldn't fail in the States (see 'Curse Of The Berts' to find out how it could). In the meantime, we merrily carried on doing the college circuit with occasional breaks to perform *Sleak* in Europe. These were gigs to behold. Unconstrained by being in Britain, the show went even more over the top. Before each performance, Judy, dressed as Jackie Kennedy in a lovely pink suit and blood on her lap, would go round with an ice-cream tray selling souvenir pieces of 'The President's head', along with sticks of 'Snuff Rock'.

Even the record sold well, but in a sense it was the end of the 'original' Albertos. When we went back on the road, Tony and Bob felt that they'd had enough, and by early 1978 had jacked it in to pursue an alternative musical career as The Mothmen, which oddly enough mutated into The Durutti Column, which very soon contained neither of them.

It was obvious that we needed replacements, and quickly. We looked around for the best musicians on the Manchester scene we could get our hands on, and finally settled on two of the more relaxed members of that community, John Scott and Captain Mog. Both of them had already tasted 'fame' – John in the Rabid houseband that had accompanied Jilted John on record and on *Top of The Pops*, and the Captain in a band called The Smirks, who were on the Berserkely label, alongside Jonathan Richman and The Modern Lovers. But the chance to play the fool with the Berts was too strong for them and on board they came.

I found myself in the rather pleasant position of having to travel quite regularly to New York to help get things organised for *Sleak* to go on over there, in between swanning around Europe living the high life.

BW

Sleak: A Fun Show About Death 157

ALBERTO Y LOST TRIOS PARANOIAS

SLEAK!
By C. P. LEE
Directed by Charlie Hanson

Once in a while a show comes along that sets the world of Showbiz talking. Shows like 'Chorus Line', 'Rocky Horror Show' and 'What Ho Pinge'.

Then of course a show may come along where people say . . . 'I had a nice piece of haddock for my tea last night' — 'Sleak' was one of those.

Here's what the papers had to say about Sleak:

Guardian: 'I had a nice piece of haddock last night.'

N.M.E.: 'I had a nice piece of haddock last night.'

Times: 'This most exciting piece of haddock.'

There are more quotes we could use, but why not judge for yourself?

Come along and see 'Sleak', marvel at the two-headed woman's struggle against the man eating barrel. Thrill to a gigantic librium crazed ape throttling a bee, or turn over this leaflet and read alternative reality tip number 38 — the show the National Theatre has never heard of, and it's arguable that 'Sleak' hasn't heard of the N.T., otherwise we wouldn't have mentioned it.

ALL SEATS BURNABLE

Photo by KLAD McNULTY

ROYAL COURT   SLOANE SQ. SW1

Snuff rock

SLEAK!
By C. P. LEE
Directed by Charlie Hanson

ALBERTO Y LOST TRIOS PARANOIAS
Michael Deeks, Judy Lloyd, Arthur Kelly and Gorden Kaye

DON'T MISS — THE RETURN OF SLEAK!
from 12th SEPTEMBER for three weeks only.

Guardian: 'FUNNIEST SHOW I'VE SEEN FOR YEARS'
Robin Denselow

Evening News: 'FUNNIEST ROCK MUSICAL SINCE THE ROCKY HORROR SHOW'

Melody Maker: 'SLEAK DESERVES TO RUN AND RUN'

Performance 8.30 a.m.
BOX OFFICE: 01-730 1745   ALL SEATS BOOKABLE

P

CHAPTER NINE
IN THE PAW OF THE PIG

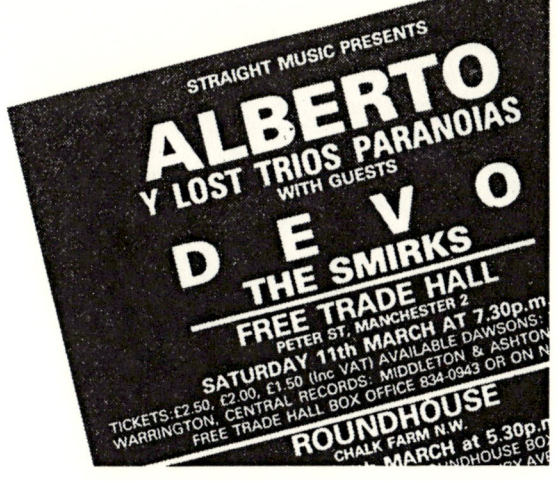

9

STRAIGHT MUSIC PRESENTS

ALBERTO
Y LOST TRIOS PARANOIAS
WITH GUESTS

D E V O
THE SMIRKS

FREE TRADE HALL
PETER ST. MANCHESTER 2
SATURDAY 11th MARCH AT 7.30p.m
TICKETS: £2.50, £2.00, £1.50 (inc VAT) AVAILABLE DAWSONS:
WARRINGTON, CENTRAL RECORDS: MIDDLETON & ASHTON
FREE TRADE HALL BOX OFFICE 834-0943 OR ON N

ROUNDHOUSE
CHALK FARM N.W.
MARCH at 5.30p.m

Throughout my career as a member of a modern day electronic beating group, travelling round the world and entertaining people with our own inimitable brand of wacky humour, it was our misfortune on a number of occasions to have been singled out by diligent customs officers from a variety of nation states and given, what I believe is termed, a right-good going over.

Considering that the nomadic Berts in their full 'on the road' glory resembled nothing less than a group of mental hospital day release patients entering a fancy-dress competition as alien life-forms from another planet, this is hardly surprising. I've recently come round to the opinion that Howard Marks probably shared lots of our journeys unbeknownst to us and, as we were being strip searched by customs officers in little rooms that all looked the same the world over, he, dressed smartly in a casual suit, would calmly breeze through the 'nothing to declare' channel with a suitcase stuffed full of kilos of the finest hashish money could buy, and not be bothered by anyone. Obviously, if we'd known that then we could have charged him a fee.

Logic and a smidgen of intelligence dictate that if you're going to smuggle something into a country you're going to try and look as inconspicuous as possible. There again, from the point of view of a customs officer, that might be a double bluff. If I look like Bozo the Clown after a week-long tequila bender, I might feel that I look so bizarre nobody's going to think I'd be stupid enough to stuff half a kilo of heroin down the front of my baggy pants, then ergo, that's exactly the time to do it! This inverted logic of the official mind appeared to hold sway pretty well each time we crossed an international border, certainly during the early part of our career. After that, meek, mild mannered John Scott became the band's official scapegoat on occasions like this. A felony compounded by his insistence on travelling with a giant rubber centipede stuffed in his cabin luggage (more of which later), and a general air of stoned insouciance brought on by a prodigious intake of alcohol rather than illicit narcotics.

The band's official maxim on drugs and customs was, 'if you can't swallow it – don't carry it', and as a result of this we were never caught doing anything illegal, only inconvenienced out of our skulls by over zealous (un)civil servants painstakingly searching the Bertmobile and our good selves for hour upon hour. I'll never forget one arrival back in the land of our birth after a European tour in 1975. A cold grey dawn and a cavernous customs shed. The way the harsh neon striplight glinted off the National Front badge worn by one of Her Majesty's finest as he asked where we'd come from. How his eyes lit up when we said we'd been to Holland, land of legal drugs and hippy highs. "I'm going to ask you all to get out of the van and stand over there," he said, gesticulating towards a long metal table. "I'll just go and get some colleagues." True to his word he returned a few seconds later with a cheerful crew of bone-headed thugs in ill-fitting uniforms, rubbing their hands together in gleeful anticipation of an imminent bust.

I was the first one to be called in for a strip search. In between chewing the couple of grams of best Nepalese Temple Ball I'd got stashed in my mouth, I attempted to explain why they weren't going to like what they were about to have unveiled in front of them. Four weeks earlier on the first night of the tour the Bertmobile had been robbed while we were playing the Tivoli Gardens in Copenhagen. The thieves (don't believe all that peace and love shit about Christiana Free State!) had made off with all our luggage, so the Berts had been forced to live and play in essentially the same clothes for a considerable time. It being very early spring meant that any attempt to wash and dry socks or underpants on hotel radiators had resulted in damp extremities for lengthy periods of the journey. My attempts to cheer everyone up with arcane bits of knowledge about Tibetan lamas who could dry wet blankets draped across their naked shoulders in sub-zero temperatures, culled from the magnificent book about Buddhist metaphysics, *Magic and Mystery In Tibet*, by Alexandra David Neal, had been met with hoots of derision by my permanently damp, permanently cold, travelling companions. But why didn't we just buy some new clothes, I hear you ask? Because basically, at that time we were earning very little money. None of us had credit cards, or if anybody did they weren't saying anything about them. The tiny per diem payment we got everyday was just about enough to cover food and drink. Kindly hippies who probably had less than we did (don't believe all that rip-off shit about Christiana Free State!) donated t-shirts and incredibly small waisted jeans that only Les could fit in because he had cancer.

The lack of a change of clothing, plus the previous three or four days having been spent more or less in the van while we played our way towards the ferry meant that we were very, very ripe. More than ripe actually. Even a depraved goat would have baulked at sexual union with any one of us. So, between trying to swallow my hash, apologising for the smell and with the 'snapping' sound of rubber gloves being pulled on hairy fists ringing in my ears, I bent over and assumed the position with an élan that only years of familiarisation with the procedure could have brought about.

My final memory of this vignette - As I was allowed to leave the room, a nauseated customs officer, a woman in fact who had been roped in to enjoy the freak show no doubt, gingerly handed me back my rancid Doc Martens, with a look on her face that indicated mild disgust mingled with hatred. With a muted air of triumph my clothes and I walked out of the room together.

One by one, bored Berts ambled into the strip search room and ambled out again, doing up buttons and zips, tying up laces and smiling at the inanity of it all. As Bruce came out last of all a thin cheer went up as we prepared to board the van. This turned into a collective groan as bone-head number one told us to stay where we were as they weren't finished with us yet. Thwarted in their attempt to nail us for what they obviously thought would be an easy bust, they'd decided to take the van to bits and call in the sniffer dogs. We waited for Rover The Wonder Dog to arrive while the rest of them circled the VW taking it in turns to push a little mirror with wheels mounted on it underneath the chassis, while other 'experts' carefully examined the upholstery, shouting in triumph, when, undoing a bunk-bed, a shower of little packages rained down on them. To be fair, we'd wondered what the smell in the van had been. We'd looked everywhere for dead things, but we'd never thought to look above our heads, and now Bruce's little secret was out.

JB Arthur Kelly looking suave

European hotel breakfasts aren't the most exciting in the world – rye bread slices, a bit of ham, cheese and maybe eggs – but they are free. In order to save a few bob, every time Bruce had gone down to the breakfast buffet he'd stashed little bits and pieces of food, mainly boiled eggs, wrapped them in paper serviettes and hidden them in various locations around the van for 'the lean times'. These 'drug parcels' that were falling on the heads of the excited customs officers were in fact very old hard boiled eggs, squashed flat and merged into soggy tissue shrouds enveloped with mould. We congratulated the officers on locating the source of the only smell that was stronger than us.

Enter Berts' Best Friend?

Finally a dog van pulled up and a rather splendid customs man in a very sharp uniform stepped out There was every indication that he'd modelled himself after 'Smithy' from *On The Buses*. After adjusting his peaked cap he went round to the back of the van and let out a very excited golden Labrador, which he led over towards us. Jimmy, who'd probably had a dog when he was a kid, leant down to pet it. "Gerroff!" yelped the dog-man, " He's very highly trained!" As the Labrador nearly licked Jimmy to death with an enthusiasm that would have put one of the Plaster Casters to shame, we wittily retorted, "So's Jimmy!" Bone-Head and his mates ushered us away from the van and made us stand in a quiet corner of the customs shed while the highly trained search began.

It's now necessary to have another quick word about the state of the interior of the Bertmobile. For quite some time through this tour and the one before that, in fact during its entire time on the road, it had become a kind of hermeneutic chamber, sealed off from the rest of the world – a compact travelling unit resembling in a bizarre way the train carriage that carried Lenin back to Russia from Switzerland, described by Winston Churchill as 'a sealed canister containing the evil bacillus of revolution'. In our case the message it contained didn't carry quite the same sense of apocalyptic imagery, more a sort of message to the youth of Europe of, 'Oh, isn't Rock boring'. Still, sealed it virtually was, and if there was any bacillus at all contained inside it, it was that of cannabis sativa smoke residue. What had once been proud, cream-coloured fake leather upholstery and Naugahyde sleeping booths was now the nicotine and dope stained vomit yellow so redolent of the average English pub. Add to that, the detritus of a tour - mashed up posters, programmes, chip wrappers, dog-eared paperbacks, cigarette ends, tin cans and empty bottles of chocolate milk, the odd sock and a flick knife or two, and you can imagine the interior. Now bear in mind that the van contained no dope at all, just the impregnation of several weeks solid smoking and you get the idea.

Well, Rover went ballistic – Rover's handler shot inside shouting words of encouragement – "Go on Rover! Seek! Seek!" but wherever Rover

GM

went it was barely a moment before Rover would bark and shoot off in another direction, yelping and foaming at the mouth in a state of complete happiness. They train the sniffer dogs by feeding them little pellets of dope when they uncover a stash, or so popular legend has it. Anyway, every time the over-excited hound started barking and sniffing and scrabbling, the customs men would dive to the spot, their antennae twitching, and tear that particular piece of the van apart. Needless to say, they didn't find anything because we'd outwitted them by unwittingly coating the entire inside of the van with a thin film of charge. Where they expected to find weights, half weights, kilos, lord knows what, they found – well, nothing, but hell, they knew something was there! They

GM

just couldn't find it. And the dog was still going berserk. They called off the search, spent a good five minutes trying to drag the freaked-out Rover from the van - if you've ever had to get a horse jacked up with methamphetamine inside a trailer (though I find it hard to believe that many of you have!), reverse that mental image and imagine how hard it was to get the dog out of our van - that overgrown puppy just wanted more of the Berts!!

After a good fifteen-minute conversation between themselves, the dog-handler and the customs man came over to us. With a look of 'we know as sure as hell you're guilty of something, but we just don't know what it is' they reluctantly told us to be on our way. They then questioned our parentage before suggesting in less than Biblical terms that we go forth and multiply. They finished off by telling us to be more careful in the future – What of? – We'd just got through one of the most rigorous strip searches I'd ever had and not one of us had been found with anything. They'd had a good four or five hours justifying their existence while Howard Marks had no doubt slipped casually ashore behind us with the entire gross national product of Columbia in his suitcases.

P Judy Lloyd sits amongst the cabbages and peas

Before going any further with this chapter I'd like to say how much customs officers have changed over the years – Now they are more intelligent, handsome and polite. Quite simply, they are a credit to our nation and seriously under funded in their fight against crime.

Tel Aviv I Done Gone

It's not just customs posts at borders that the Berts manfully grappled with in their time, but also security at airports. Obviously this increased exponentially throughout the 1970s as insane terrorist organisations attempted to alter world opinion by interfering with my travel plans. John Scott, as I mentioned earlier, caused many a fuss at several international airports due to his insistence on carrying his personal props inside his

In the Paw of the Pig   167

hand luggage (yet nought compared to Bruce, as you'll see shortly). An airport security x-ray image of a two-foot long rubber centipede is

JB Another tour, another radio interview

guaranteed to arouse curiosity in the most idle of bystanders, especially when sandwiched in with a couple of pairs of socks, Ross Russell's biography of Charlie Parker, *Bird Lives*, 200 Marlboro and four cans of extra strong beer. John's rather laid back approach at justifying the centipede's presence to assembled groups of bewildered security staff weren't guaranteed to help either. "Er, it's for my head, you know".

How on earth this wriggling, fluorescent rubber replica of one of the most freaky creatures on the planet could be 'for my head' remained a mystery to even the most erudite operative in the airport security business. If they'd been fluent in what the Berts termed 'Johnspeak' they would have sussed instantly that he simply meant that at a certain part of the show he would pretend to be the Statue of Liberty by wrapping the centipede round his head like a crown, drape a ragged old cloth round himself, with one hand holding up a switched-on Eveready torch, whilst in the other hand holding the paperback copy of *Bird Lives* close to his chest and standing stock still. While he did this he somehow managed to play saxophone as well, but none of us could figure how he did that - probably while we weren't looking. As the queue at airports got longer behind us, the security staff would look imploringly at John for more information. This was occasionally forthcoming, delivered in his own inimitable manner, for John was known in those days to take a drink or two before a flight, after a flight, and during a flight (CP to John. "John, the lads have asked me to have a word with you about your drinking." – John, "Oh, great, cheers - I'll have a pint!"). However ...

Intermission

Andrew and Peter at Blackhill had come up with several plans which would have been amusing if they hadn't asked the Berts to carry them out. For example, a tour of the Costa del Sol nightclubs in 1975 - Pretty good idea except for the fact that Franco was still in charge of Spain - "But they're crying out for English bands to play over there!" "Yes, but we're anarchists!" - Then there was the "Roy Harper's going to play in the Lebanon, why don't you?" "Erm, whereabouts?" - "The Beirut Hilton - Honestly, it only gets shelled occasionally!" – Not to mention, the "They may have killed the Miami Showband, but this time you'll knock 'em dead Irish tour!", which for some bizarre reason we actually undertook.

The PA gear blew up in Belfast shortly after a gig started and I adlibbed a line, "The gear's blown up and no one's accepted responsibility!" - There were a few seconds of stunned silence, then a wave of laughter that really broke the ice. On the same tour Black Paul the Roady was blown up in an on-stage accident that the Dublin A&E wrongly assumed was the IRA but that's another story.

P Simon Tommy White looking cool

Back To The Front

Just after we'd got back from the States in early 1981 Andrew had another proposition - a week-long residency in Tel Aviv, at a club called The Penguin (as described in Chapter 6). What takes place next is at Ben Gurion Airport when our residency ended and we were about to fly home. We knew that airport security in Israel was tight. You'll remember that Ari, the former head of the Tel Aviv drug squad was our host in Israel and he had warned us that we would encounter difficulties getting through and onto our flight as special precautions were always being taken to stop Palestinian guerrillas from planting devices on unsuspecting tourists. But you'll also remember that we were emerging from our tequila-induced haze from life in the Tel Aviv Hilton ... so despite the advice, we were blissfully unaware of the carnage that was about to follow.

It was a relatively quiet Monday morning as we shuffled shambolically towards the security area carrying hangovers as big as our hand luggage. Ari bid us farewell as we checked in for the El Al London flight. Things were going well, too well ...

At the security desk was a young Sabra girl in Israeli military uniform, blouse, mini skirt, knee boots and her hair in bunches. An Uzi machine gun hung from her shoulders. Her luxurious black hair and pouting lips, oh well, you get the idea ... She was the source of a thousand knock ups. To a man, the Albertos shuffled nervously, giggling, bowing their heads and looking uselessly about. The usual questions followed, "Where are you going?" "Did anybody give you anything to carry on the flight?" "Anything no matter how small and insignificant?" We all grinned sheepishly and replied in the negative, we were clean and proud of it. We didn't want to inconvenience this rather charming young lady and were all eager to please her. She asked what should have been her final question – "Is there anything in your hand luggage that I should know about?"

John was first of course, and after she'd asked him the usual questions she put her hands inside his bag and pulled out the centipede. It quivered in her hands as she examined it, rather like we would have done if she'd been examining us, when for some bizarre reason she seemed happy with his explanation as to the rubber insect's purpose. John passed through the security line and waited for us on the other side of the desk. Bruce was next.

In what passed for his most debonair, devil-may-care, nonchalant walk, Bruce sauntered over to the desk and the sexy Sabra soldier. He looked like a very fussy camel choosing a cream cake. "This is my bag," he said, tossing a filthy black canvas holdall onto her desk. "I packed it all myself this morning". She looked at it dispassionately like a forensic pathologist might look at a corpse. "Is there anything in there I should know about?"

she asked. Bruce began to giggle like a naughty schoolboy. "Er, no... I packed it myself ... Er, this morning ... No"

Without taking her eyes off Bruce's face she plunged her arm deep into his bag like a vet birthing a calf. She rummaged around for a bit like it

NEAR MISSES OF THE FOURTH KIND

might be Siamese twins and then came out with a Sam Brown army belt complete with a pistol holster. Bruce grinned insanely and turned bright scarlet, his chest started heaving. For those of us in the know, this was always a prelude to an asthma attack. Things were looking good. Jimmy, Simon and I nudged one another. Captain Mog looked quizzically out of his hangover-induced fog as the soldier lady held up Bruce's gun-belt like a schoolteacher might hold up a used condom.

Suddenly, around the airport departure lounge things changed. A cleaner threw down his broom and produced an Uzi from his mop bucket. An elderly American couple, the husband in a wheelchair, suddenly flung off the shackles of age and stood training their machine guns on us. Several Orthodox Rabbis flung themselves to the floor brandishing the kind of hardware that Bruce Willis would give his eye teeth for. This was how Israeli security forces protected their airport - by taking no chances. Bruce Mitchell was by now an even deeper shade of red, approaching purple, wheezing furiously and stammering, "This morning ... packed it ... me ... " A rictus grin was fixed on his face. I was in hysterics so Jimmy stepped forward and tried to explain that we were a band, it was part of the stage show. We'd just played a week's residency at The Penguin Club. At the name of the venue she seemed to understand and relaxed a little. "Oh, Ari," she said, as if it all made sense. I guess everybody in Tel Aviv knew his name. Still, she didn't let down her arm and the gun belt hung in the air like a question mark over our futures. The cleaner, the geriatrics and the Rabbis still had us firmly in their sights.

Slowly putting the gun belt down she asked Bruce if he had anything else in his bag that she should know about. Bruce tried to speak, but it was hard going because he wasn't just having an asthma attack, he was, like us, almost doubled up with laughter, "No ... nothing ... this morning ... packed it ... me ..." His hands gripped her desk in an attempt to remain upright. His Ronald Coleman act had failed long since and now he was out for a sympathy vote on account of his inability to breathe. Well, that's the way we figured it. We'd never seen him so red.

Once more our military minx plunged courageously into the gaping orifice of Bruce's stage bag. After rummaging around for a bit longer her face took on a look of horrified bewilderment. She looked sternly at Bruce who had begun to sway like he was about to pass out. "Me ... Packed ... Morning ..." he gibbered, grinning like a psychotic chimp at a particularly manic tea party. She withdrew her hand and held up a plastic see-through hand-grenade, also part of the act. Fingers on the assembled triggers tightened. Sweat poured down brows. She put it to one side to a soundtrack of clicking magazines and gun-bolts and then thrust her hand back inside the bag. To her added bewilderment the next item she produced was a pair of plaster hands from a shop mannequin. Everybody stared at them with rapt attention. Well we knew that they were just another stage prop - Bruce would fix a pair of drumsticks into the two plaster hands and then stick them on to two broomsticks and by holding these he could extend his fake arms at a crucial juncture during his drum solo. He had a reach of about ten feet on either side. He even had a suit with specially elongated arms to accommodate them. It was a masterpiece of comic art. This time though it might be a masterpiece that was lost on the honey babe of the Israeli Army, as voted for by the panting, slobbering massed ranks of the Albertos' army.

We fell silent. Even Bruce, for that moment, managed to stop wheezing and breathlessly clutched the desk.

John looked quizzically from the other side of the barrier and opened a can of beer.

The gun toting 'members of the public' took a sharp intake of breath as the plaster hands were raised aloft by Sabra girl.

She looked round at her back-up squad.

In the style of Sylvester Stallone, we were surrounded by one motherfucking load of weaponry now trained on the offending appendage.

"It's okay," she said, cool as a cucumber, "It's not armed."

Pop Party's Passport Package Plugs The People's Pipeline!

We used to have to drive to West Berlin via East Germany when we were touring, and boy! Were those sensational times ... Well, no ... In fact they were, generally speaking, mind-excruciatingly boring by dint of the ritual shakedown you got at the border crossing into East Germany. Acres of trucks and cars waiting in sidings while the Grepo, soldiers and sundry other gun-toting, uniformed, acne-ridden kids stamped up and down the lines of vehicles in the snow. Always the snow. I don't think we ever toured there in the summer. It was always grey and raining, or grey and snowing. Always bitterly cold. Anybody who has had the misfortune to have visited the coastal resort of Southport in the North West of England on an off-season Sunday in the winter of, ooh, let's say,

1963, will immediately read my description of East Berlin in the mid to late 1970s and feel they know the place, except Southport wouldn't have had the bullet marks and shell holes that still adorned a lot of the East Berlin buildings twenty years after the war.

God, it was depressing in every sense. Officials at the border never failed to miss a trick to collect a few Deutchmarks 'entry fee' as they picked up your passports which were popped into a bundle, then stuffed into one of those antiquated pipe systems and propelled by compressed air to a kind of giant watchtower that dominated the car park. Into it and out of it poured lines of field grey figures, like droves of worker ants busying themselves around the corpse of a bluebottle.

Usually you'd expect to wait for an hour or more while your passports and visas were processed, not that there ever seemed to be any sense of urgency on the part of the People's Army to aid your progress through the People's Socialist Republic. Hey, we were people too! On one particular occasion, the wait seemed to be even more prolonged than usual. Occasionally small gaggles of soldiers would wander over towards the Bertmobile and stare at us from a few yards away. Other groups came and went to the pipeline, gesticulated and wandered off. Eventually, quite a few of them appeared to be settling in there, making signals with their arms to the command tower. One particularly inquisitive trooper came

P Backstage Royal Albert Hall - Bandages? Don't ask ...

and rapped on the side door of the van. When we pulled it open he took a step back and levelled his Kalashnikov straight at us. He looked Russian and he looked mean, older than the others and with possibly less acne.

Still holding his gun in front of him he poked his head inside the van and looked at us. Bruce nibbled nonchalantly on a hard boiled egg and grinned at him. I put down my copy of *Man's Rise To Civilisation* by Peter Farb, and woke up Tony Bowers. I didn't want him to get shot without knowing about it first - he would have hated to miss it.

With a rueful look on his face the gun-toting Ivan finally spoke. I don't know what had given it away, maybe the guitar cases, clothes and long hair, but he said simply – "Rock 'n' Roll?" We nodded. "Ah, Rock 'n' Roll!" flipping his Kalashnikov round and strumming it like a guitar - "Elvis Presley!" - We all humoured him by pretending that his hip swivelling impression of the King was the bees knees, quite simply one of the best we'd ever seen, possibly even better than Presley himself. He suddenly stopped and stood to attention when a voice barked out a command behind him. There stood an officer looking the very model of what an East German/Russian officer should look like if he'd been sent along by central casting. He was clutching our passport bundle and didn't seem to be very happy about it.

After a few minutes of conversation with Bob Harding, the Bert's resident linguist, it transpired that 'alles in ordnung', all was in order with our papers. The reason it had taken so long to process them was that our bundle was so big it had blocked the compressed air pipeline and teams of East German army technicians had had to work their way slowly along it until it could be opened and the package retrieved. As a result, hundreds of people were now hours behind schedule and it was a thoroughly miserable caravan of vehicles that finally snaked off into the communist twilight.

The Curious Case Of The Kipper Tie

As you will have read earlier, an essential part of Bruce's stage attire was his (in)famous giant, wooden kipper tie. On the front was a picture of a naked woman. On the reverse side, to avoid accusations of sexism, was a picture of a naked man, usually culled from the centrefold in *Playgirl* magazine. It was this seemingly inoffensive little publication that was to lead to yet another hairy little border incident, this time going into East Berlin from the West.

In the Paw of the Pig   175

We were performing a short residency in a converted cinema called The Quartier Latin. It seemed like an ideal opportunity for a quick trip through Checkpoint Charlie, to view life behind the Iron Curtain. Disregarding the advice of early Rock explorers who'd told us to take suitcases stuffed with Levi jeans and Animals LPs, perfect bartering fodder to the Popular Culture starved youth of the Eastern Bloc, without a thought we hopped in the VW and drove down the road playing at being characters in a John La Carre novel.

It didn't take us long to get through the Western sector and pretty soon we parked up at yet another security checkpoint having our Pop people's passports and visas checked yet again. As we were only day-trippers we naively thought the process might be a little shorter than usual, but the East Germans were nothing if not thorough and it was decided that they wanted to search the van anyway. We weren't bothered. This time the van was clean, as indeed, so were we, clothes, bodies and everything. Let them do their worst. Let them bring on their finest bureaucratic sawdust Caesars. We were impregnable in our righteousness. Nothing could phase us now ... It was then that we first noticed Ilse Koch.

We'd all been brought up on the stereotypical cliché of the female Eastern European athlete, you know the kind – 275 pound women shot-putters with stubble on their chins and biceps like ham-hocks. Well, here she was in all her blazing glory, steaming towards us like a battleship leaving harbour, carrying all before her. I'd swear her knuckles were touching her knees and that she was all of six foot tall. Her face looked like a bulldog sucking a wasp. To say we were unnerved would be putting it mildly. She supervised a team of evil henchmen who bowed to her every bidding. They pulled out seats, they poked behind tyres. They even had one of those mirrors on a trolley, just like their British counterparts, so they could look under the van. We gazed in fascinated awe as she ordered her men hither and yon, steadfast in their determination to stem the filthy tide of capitalistic excess reaching their country.

> **ALBERTO Y** Lost Trios Paranoias have lost two of their members — Tony Bowers (bass) and Bob Harding (keyboards), both of whom quit the band last week. The remaining five say they are close to finding replacements.

Suddenly she let out a roar of triumph and her cohort fell back. They then moved in again like jackals around a dying gazelle. We all looked at one another in a state of bewildered shock. What the Hell could she have found? What was the phone number of the British Embassy? Would we end up being swapped on a bridge over the Charlotte River, for some effete art historian? She hauled her gigantic ass out of the van and her jackboots thundered out a tattoo of terror on the East German cobbles. She marched straight up to us and thrust out a battered copy of Playgirl - "Whose is?!" she thundered.

If ever there was a time to show these jumped-up totalitarian robots what freedom and democracy really were, how we free-born Englishmen would refuse to wilt under the combined pressure of their guns and labour camps and stand united in our defiance of their perverted Marxist ideology, this wasn't it. "It was him!" we all shouted at once pointing at Bruce who, as usual, started to have an asthma attack.

The guards all started talking amongst themselves. I could make out words like 'decadent' and 'homosexual'. Ilse Koch turned towards us. "You may all go now – But zis – zis is confiscated and vill be destroyed!" she bellowed and heaved to starboard back to her hut. We trooped back to the van cheerfully laughing and prodding Bruce. As we drove slowly out of Checkpoint Charlie I caught a glimpse of her carefully placing the offending magazine in the bottom drawer of her desk. A very satisfied smile was crossing her face.

The Tale Of The No Armed Mountie

During the late 1970s I was doing quite a bit of hopping backwards and forwards across the Atlantic making arrangements for the staging of *Sleak* in New York. Through the auspices of Joseph Papp and the Dodgers Production Company I'd somehow managed to find myself with a multiple entry visa and a temporary work permit. In the summer of 1979 I was invited to Banff College of Arts in Canada, where the guy who was going to direct the American version of *Sleak*, Des McAnuff was teaching summer school. Somehow they wangled it so I was to be a writer in residence. Little did I realise when I set off from Manchester on a fine cloudy morning what dangers lay ahead of me.

At the risk of being boring I'm going to have to explain things chronologically. Firstly, train to London where, just to keep things interesting, Blackhill had arranged for me to audition for the part of leader of a gang of Hell's Angels in the hit TV show *The Professionals*. I turned up at the production company's office where within minutes both sides realised I wasn't the guy they were looking for. They'd seen a four-year-old photo of me dressed up as a greaser and now I was sporting a crop. Added to this was the rather important fact that the character led a motorcycle gang, and even to this very day I've steadfastly never learned to drive. The odds against me becoming a TV villain grew every greater and finally the TV people 'let me go', though they were very polite about all their time being wasted and I was able to blag a cab off them to keep my second appointment of the day. Much better this one - a highly unofficial meet-up with Frank Zappa.

He was playing that night at Wembley. I knew he liked some of the stuff John Scott and I had been doing on Absurd Records and a tentative meeting had been arranged by mutual friends. Zappa was doing his soundcheck when I arrived and I was ushered in to find within minutes that I was being auditioning for The Mothers. At least I think I was. Zappa didn't speak much, just watched and listened - one minute I was singing *Camarillo Brillo*, the next I was doing *Brown Shoes* and when the songs were finished I went on my way. When I got back from the States an opportunity to do a tour had been made but I was far too busy fucking up the Berts' career to be a very small cog in somebody else's ego trip. At least that's what I told myself later.

A night getting wrecked was followed by yet another journey, this time to Heathrow where I caught a flight to New York. I arrived in the Apple where the humidity hit me like a wet, warm blanket, checked into my hotel and then set out to visit one of the backers of *Sleak*. I arrived at his apartment and enthusiastically shook hands with the guy who opened the cab door for me. He politely explained that he was the concierge and showed me the elevator. I eventually found myself with a really strange man whose name I can't remember, nor do I wish to. He kept asking me, did I get a lot of pussy in England? Did chicks like, make out? It must be groovy being in a band, all those groupies? I didn't have the energy to tell him that our groupies were usually tubby blokes with beards who wanted to know if we were as much into the *Goon Show* as they were, and had we watched the last series of *Monty Python*? Us pull groupies! We were more likely to pull a ligament.

I managed to escape his evil clutches and got back to the hotel where I forced myself to watch re-runs of Groucho Marx on *You Bet Your Life* until I drifted off only to wake up at about six in the morning. I noodled about for a bit until it was time to go to the airport again, this time to get a flight to Calgary for Banff. As I flew West across the North American continent I realised that I was pretty bushed so decided to get stuck into a few bottles of wine to liven myself up a bit. I didn't need to, the weather was going to do that for me.

We were quite near to Calgary when the electrical storm hit. Sheets and streaks of lightning flashed around the plane. The plane began bucking and broncking. Some people screamed. So did I. My wine had fallen over! Then the pilot announced that we were going to have to fly around the storm and that meant extra time on our journey. His apologies for the delay cut no ice with me. Fly through the fucker! I thought. I've got a bus to catch. The last bus of the day from Calgary to Banff to be precise.

I was cutting it fine already. I glanced at my watch and did some quick mental configurations. Then I crossed my fingers.

We eventually landed. The way I figured it I had about forty minutes to clear customs and immigration. It was going to be tight, but if I didn't panic I could just make it. Everyone trouped inside the airport terminal and headed for immigration. I was feeling pretty cool. It was then that they stopped me. A group of guys were watching us as we filed in. They picked me and a handful of Iranians and asked us to stand in a corner. Everyone else went through and got their baggage.

GM Captain Mog steps in on Bass

I checked my appearance. Was that what had got me pulled? As far as I was concerned I looked pretty sharp. My off-white linen suit had been hand tailored in Hong Kong. Admittedly I'd bought it from an Oxfam shop in Manchester, but it nearly fitted me! My off-white sun hat was sitting pretty on top of my neatly coiffed head, perfectly offsetting my Raybans. The three-day stubble on my face might have seemed a little out of sorts, but not on the face of the seasoned traveller I tried hard to convince myself I looked like, and it matched perfectly the crumpled state of my suit. When I looked at my t-shirt I had an inkling of what may have given them their suspicions about me. It was a reproduction of Gerald Scarfe's cover design for Hunter S Thompson's *Fear and Loathing In Las Vegas*. And I'd spilt wine down it! Just as I'd begun to reflect on this I was ushered into the room of a Mr Maclean, of the Canadian Immigration Services.

Now I was tired, I'd been drinking, I'd been on the go for days and I had serious jetlag, but none of that excuses what happened next. After a few innocuous questions establishing my bona fides and looking at the letter of introduction from Banff, Mr Maclean asked if I had any friends or relatives in Canada. My mouth, which was always too fast for my brain said something like, "You must be joking!" His polite smile faded as did the time I had left to catch my bus. He was, he said, going to carefully review my position. With that he left me sitting in the room idly gazing at the travel posters up on the walls. "You'll get a great welcome in Canada"

GM Berts on the road in their mobile library

one of them read. "Yeah, fucking right you will," I thought. My reverie was disturbed by Mr Maclean coming back into the room and sitting himself down at his desk. Puffing laconically on his pipe he studied me for a moment or two before pronouncing judgement. "We're not sure we want your type in Canada Mr Lee." he drawled. "However, because of your invitation we're going to let you in … under certain conditions. You will report to the Mounted Police station in Banff once a week and notify us if you decide to visit anywhere else in Canada. Is that clear?"

Clear? Oh yes, it was clear all right. And I didn't give a toss as long as I could catch my bus and get the hell out of Calgary. "When you've collected your bags you may proceed through customs," he continued. I murmured a muted set of thanks and goodbyes and went off down the hall towards reclaim. Thank Christ! There was my bag. Now for customs.

I'm clean, it should be a breeze. I joined the line of recidivists who were waiting for processing and realised that the gig was up. I experienced a kind of reverse déjà-vu. Let's call it préjà-vu - instead of going back in time though, I went forward - in an instant I knew exactly what was going to take place over the next thirty minutes or so.

There were three benches in the customs hall. Three customs officers were on duty - a woman and two men. One of the men had no arms, that is to say he had on a light blue customs officer shirt with short sleeves, out of which poked two stumps. He was talking to a passenger. From within the recesses of my new, super transcendental state I rationalised that he was working as a customs officer despite his apparent physical limitations for the job because of Canada's liberal equality laws. As a reasonable human being, I didn't and don't think there's anything wrong with that, in fact I applaud whoever gave him the job. Even if he couldn't.

I also knew that no matter where I was in the queue, whichever arbitrary position fate had put me in, I was going to end up with him. I could have been first, third, or seventh - he could have been one of twenty - our fates were intertwined, our destinies locked together - He was armless, I was almost legless. And sure enough, I found myself standing in front of him. As he uttered his opening gambit of, "Have you anything to declare?" I tried really hard to suppress the rising tide of laughter that was threatening to engulf me. Grinning like an idiot and attempting to breath normally and yet hold my breath at the same time in order not to dissolve in hysterics, I managed a weak shake of the head and a muffled, "No". "Then you wouldn't mind opening your bag would you sir?" he parried, his face hardening.

I unzipped my leather travel bag and held it open as he glanced inside. "Now. Would you mind searching your bag sir?" That was it! Perfect! Exactly the line that I'd heard in my state of préjà-vu, and I knew now that there was no way I was going to make my bus. I began to slowly take items from my bag. When I reached my (little used) shaving kit, the situation was cranked up another notch on the absurdity meter. "Would you mind unscrewing the bottom of your shaving brush please sir?" he ordered. I did as he asked and showed him that there was nothing hidden inside. "And could you squeeze out some of your toothpaste please?" Again I complied, barely able to stand upright because of the suppressed laughter welling up inside me. I was flashing on the appalling idea of him being dissatisfied with the thoroughness of my self-searching capabilities and had an horrendous vision of him taking me into a little room to perform an anal search. It had also occurred to me that a true surrealist would, at this point, have planted himself, but I was totally clean and therefore couldn't make the supreme Bretonesque gesture.

Finally I was expelled into the neon glare of the arrivals terminal, all my trials though sure not over. I now needed a hotel as it was definitely too late for any more travelling, and used one of the courtesy phones that waited there for me. A whole heap of tantalisingly named premises offered themselves up - Moose View - the Stampede Lodge - the Longhorn Hotel and Diner - Jesuzz! Would the torture never stop?!? Shell-shocked, battered and exhausted I dialled the Calgary Hilton and then sat down to await my complimentary mini-bus.

After checking in I got to my room and fell asleep fully clothed on the giant bed, only to snap out awake at about five in the morning. Any hopes of a good start to the day were pre-empted by finding out that room service was off and breakfast didn't start being served until seven, so I had to content myself by sitting in my room drinking tap water and watching Canadian Film Board documentaries about the mistreatment of the indigenous Canadian Indians. It would be fair to say that I was beginning to feel quite emotional, the more so later when I got down to the breakfast room and found that it was staffed almost entirely to a man by native Canadians who all bore a startling resemblance to the character of 'Chief' in *One Flew Over The Cuckoo's Nest*. Having just watched several programmes about how badly the whites had treated them, there I was, another interloper in their country, demanding more coffee and eggs over easy. By the time I left the restaurant my misery quota was way over the limit.

The next coach to Banff was at ten, which is how, at nine-thirty, I found myself in a bar next to the bus station. I was quietly enjoying a bottle of Moulson beer, when a long-hair at the next table began to engage me in conversation. Where was I from? Where was I going? He, it transpired, was an American hiding out in Canada in case President Carter reinstated the draft because of all the shit going down with Iran. Then he pulled his chair right up to mine and looked me square in the eye.

"You ever have any trouble with niggers in England?"

"No ..." I stammered. "We don't have any problems with black people."

"I said niggers!!" he shouted, leaping up and knocking over his chair. In a flash he'd pulled out a bowie knife and had me pinned to the wall. A hundred Westerns I'd watched flashed before my eyes.

"I said niggers!!" he shrieked again as a gigantic hand fell on his shoulder and pulled him away from me. A huge Indian, the barman, held the furious draft dodger by the neck.

'Chief' turned to me and said, "I don't know who you are mister, but if I were you I'd get out of here right away." - And you can rest assured that I didn't need telling twice.

Anyway, I got to Banff - got altitude sickness - it took me nearly a week to work out why I was struggling so hard to raise a glass of beer to my lips - survived being put in a log cabin half way up a mountain - met a bunch of arty/actor/writer people - and finally it was time to leave Canada. I assumed that this would be comparatively straightforward, but once more the gods smirked down on me ... Even more digression here, but I'm on a flow and it's essential to the story ...

I'd brought Des, the director, a gift. At a festival earlier in the year some crazy theatre group were doing their thing around the festival site. One of their schticks was selling do-it-yourself laser beam kits. These consisted of a length of nylon fishing line, two drawing pins and instructions of how to pin them up, all enclosed in little cellophane packets. I bought a stack of them and gave them to people as presents. I'd brought one over to Canada inside an antique Oxo tin, so the drawing pins wouldn't scratch anything. After I'd given Des his kit he reciprocated by laying a lid of best Columbian grass on me for use when I got back to the States. This I duly put inside the Oxo tin. "You won't have any trouble at Customs," he reassured me. "Who'd think anybody was carrying anything from Canada to America?"

My journey back began as badly as my journey there. Up at six to catch the bus that would take me to the airport. No coffee shop open in Banff, me with a thirst you could photograph and a water tap in the gents' toilet that was so disgusting even with a mouth drier than a Welsh Methodist Chapel on a Sunday. I gave it a miss. Once again I was clock watching. The New York flight was at mid-day. But still, all I had to do was get off the coach, check in and board the flight. No problem. You never get searched leaving a country ... do you?

Well, if you're me, of course you do. And here's how it all came to be – Get off bus with plenty of time. Grab a cup of coffee and go to check in. Check in. Pass cleanly through security and before I can breath a sigh of relief get confronted with a huge sign that says - "In order to speed your entry into the United States, American customs are now situated in this airport." - Yes, that's right, in this airport, in Canada, and, as it happens, right in front of me.

I bent down pretending to tie my shoelace and unzipped my bag and surreptitiously took out the Oxo tin, removed the dope, whispered it a fond farewell and chucked it in a garbage bin. Now clean, I made my way towards the American customs officer who was courteously letting everyone through. As I strode past him as cheerfully as I could given the circumstances, he called out to me, "Have you anything to declare, sir?"

I made a mental note to ditch my *Fear and Loathing* t-shirt as soon as I could be bothered, and replied, "Nothing" After eyeing me up for a second or two he said, "Then you wouldn't mind if I searched you, would you?"

"Nope. No problem at all," I told him as he led me into a familiar looking room at the side of the lounge.

I stood there and hummed while he poked through my bag. He pulled out my copy of Joseph Campbell's *Hero With A Thousand Faces* and held it upside down while he flicked through the pages. Only concepts for George Lucas movies fell out. Suddenly his eyes lit up. "And what have we here?", he glared triumphantly, holding up the battered old Oxo tin. I groaned inwardly.

"It's an Oxo tin," I replied. "An old one," I added helpfully.

"And what's an 'Oxo tin' for?" he enquired, six thousand miles away from the reality of an English Sunday roast dinner.

"It's for keeping cubes of beef stock in," I smiled weakly.

"And do you keep cubes of beef stock in it?" he snorted.

JB The multi-talented John Scott

"No. Do-it-yourself laser beam kits." I knew then that any semblance of control over the situation that I might once have possessed was now sliding irrevocably down the u-bend of the universe. I'd lost it.

"Do you know what I think, Mr Lee?" he shouted, triumphantly holding the tin in front of him like a conjuror. "I think you use it for containing marijuana!" With a dextrous flourish he pulled the lid off the tin and thrust it towards me. When he realised that I wasn't exactly quaking in my boots he held the tin up to his nose and sniffed deeply. I guess it must have reeked of the Columbian, but he was buggered because there wasn't actually any in there. He knew that and I knew that. Outside, in the departure lounge, I heard the last call for my flight.

Six hours later, after one of the most rigorous strip searches I've ever had, and after having had to buy a new ticket, I finally boarded a flight to New York. When I got back there it was a hundred degrees, maniacs were raging up and down the streets looking for Arabs to beat up, hookers were propositioning drunks and junkies, and boy it was good to get back home.

10

CHAPTER TEN
GUERILLAS IN THE MIST

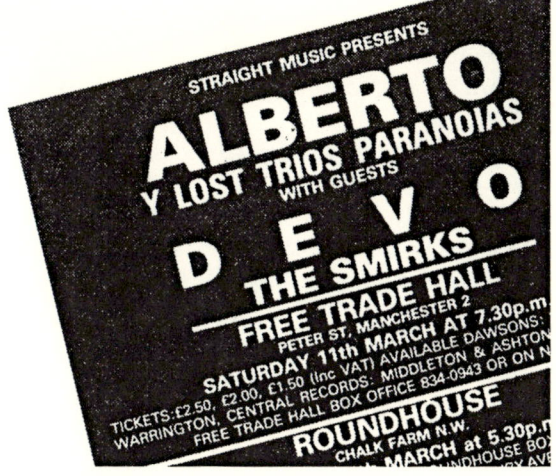

STRAIGHT MUSIC PRESENTS

ALBERTO Y LOST TRIOS PARANOIAS
WITH GUESTS

DEVO
THE SMIRKS

FREE TRADE HALL
PETER ST. MANCHESTER 2
SATURDAY 11th MARCH AT 7.30p.m.
TICKETS: £2.50, £2.00, £1.50 (Inc VAT) AVAILABLE DAWSONS;
WARRINGTON, CENTRAL RECORDS: MIDDLETON & ASHTON
FREE TRADE HALL BOX OFFICE 834-0943 OR ON N

ROUNDHOUSE
CHALK FARM N.W.
MARCH at 5.30p.m.

The following anecdotes are certified genuine and may be used without license for re-telling in pubs, living rooms, and at dinner parties, but not on oil-rigs. If you wish you may substitute your name for mine, though there is no guarantee that your friends or colleagues will find them in any way amusing.

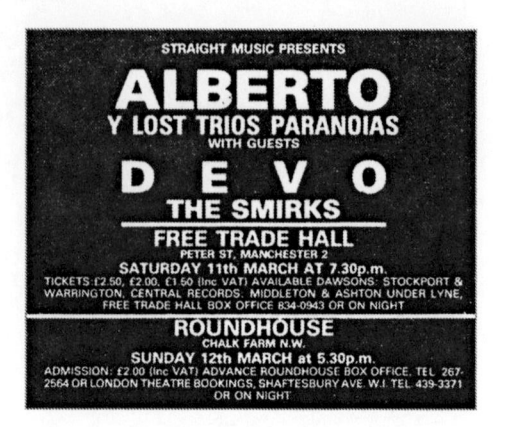

> STRAIGHT MUSIC PRESENTS
> **ALBERTO**
> **Y LOST TRIOS PARANOIAS**
> WITH GUESTS
> **D E V O**
> **THE SMIRKS**
> FREE TRADE HALL
> PETER ST, MANCHESTER 2
> SATURDAY 11th MARCH AT 7.30p.m.
> TICKETS £2.50, £2.00, £1.50 (Inc VAT) AVAILABLE DAWSONS: STOCKPORT & WARRINGTON, CENTRAL RECORDS: MIDDLETON & ASHTON UNDER LYNE, FREE TRADE HALL BOX OFFICE 834-0943 OR ON NIGHT
> ROUNDHOUSE
> CHALK FARM N.W.
> SUNDAY 12th MARCH at 5.30p.m.
> ADMISSION: £2.00 (Inc VAT) ADVANCE ROUNDHOUSE BOX OFFICE, TEL 267-2564 OR LONDON THEATRE BOOKINGS, SHAFTESBURY AVE. W.I. TEL 439-3371 OR ON NIGHT

New York Stories

When I was a young man, two women in particular held an erotic hold over my fantasies. Both were blonde and both had foreign accents. The first one was Nico, chanteuse with the Velvet Underground, and then subsequently, a solo performer. Her Gotterdammerung vocals and mysterious eyes had filled me with adolescent desire ever since I first saw her in Andy Warhol's film *Chelsea Girls*.

The second woman to colonise my libido at that time was almost a facsimile of Nico, Anita Pallenberg. Her up-front sexuality in Donald Cammell's and Nic Roeg's *Performance* knocked my socks sideways and left me with a drool splattered chin.

Cut to New York ten years later and a rather more mature CP Lee, with a full complement of Albertos in tow, is working hard with theatre director Des McAnuff getting *Sleak* ready for its opening in the Big Apple.

Our rehearsal space was in a small adjunct of Warhol's Factory, just around the corner from The Chelsea hotel, opposite a Blarney Stone bar and a Laundromat. John Scott and I had already had a very strange time one afternoon in the Blarney Stone. John, who was facing the window, suddenly looked quite piqued. I asked him what was up.

"It's alright - It's nothing, man" John replied, not quite convincingly. We carried on talking. He winced again.

"I just saw a tomato walk past the window."

I turned around and couldn't see anything out of the ordinary. I was checking John's glass when he said – "Look! Now! Quick!"

I turned around in time to see a giant green pepper walk past the bar. It was okay then, we'd both seen them. I was transported back to Manchester in 1971 and Martin Hannett and I were drinking in the Student Union bar on Oxford Road. It was three o'clock closing in the afternoons back then and as I stayed on to talk to somebody else, Martin said goodbye and left. A few minutes later he came back in ashen faced. "I've just seen an elephant" he said.

We all knew that with Martin's penchant for chemical recreation it was possible he thought he saw an elephant, but he was obviously quite shocked. He dismissed our casual enquiries about the colour of the elephant so we went outside to see for ourselves. When we reached the steps of the union there was indeed an elephant stood in the middle of the road. And a few moments later a bunch of clowns and a ringmaster arrived and shooed the elephant onwards. They were advertising a circus.

Now, in New York, it became apparent that giant vegetables were advertising something or other in similar fashion and as I had learned a valuable lesson I could reassure John - Never immediately dismiss anything anybody sees, because there's probably money behind it somewhere ... However, I digress.

Later that afternoon a few of us were taking a drink before going back into the little Factory theatre and undertaking our first proper dress-rehearsal. Andrew came in looking quite excited.

"I hope you don't mind, boys, but there's going to be a small audience this afternoon. There'll be a couple of journalists and Nico and Anita Pallenberg have asked if they could drop by."

What!?! All my youthful fantasies came flooding back. Nico and Anita Pallenberg were going to come and watch me?! Oh joy!

All the way through the dress-rehearsal I kept peering out into the auditorium, but it was too dark and I couldn't make out any of our guests. The occasional snigger, or laugh came back at us from the pitch black, but nothing I could immediately recognise as being 'Germanic'. I'd just have to wait for the show to be over before I could meet the two proud beauties.

Finally Jimmy managed to kill himself and the rehearsal finished. I was about to rush into the auditorium when Des said it was time for us to 'get our notes'.

"You must be mad," I told him. "I've waited all my life for this moment. You can give me my notes later." And with that I shot off in search of the Teutonic goddesses.

The lights in the hall were now on and I searched avidly for the objects of my affection. A couple of people were talking at the back of the room, both guys. Couldn't be them then. Two old bag ladies were sat mid-way down the rows of seats, chatting and rummaging through carrier bags. Who'd let them in, I wondered as I looked at them more closely and, with a sinking heart, realised they weren't bag ladies at all but Nico and Anita. They looked fat because they were. The slim, sylph-like figures that had got them both jobs in the 1960s as international models were gone, or buried beneath jackets, overcoats and cardigans. As they looked at me I saw their faces were bloated with a heroin sheen, their eyes blank and wasted. Their once beautiful blonde hair was lank and straggly, their once elegant hands like pig's trotters. I said nothing as they stood up to leave with a great rustling noise, gathering up their bags and heaving themselves out of their seats. I went back to get my notes off Des and to meditate on age, drugs and desire.

Dustin Doesn't Live Here Any More

I first went to New York with Bruce on a fact-finding mission in 1977, during the peak of the 'Summer of Sam' madness. The moment we stepped onto the sidewalk outside Kennedy Airport the heat and humidity hit us like a warm, wet blanket. No one who's been there can ever forget their first sight of the Manhattan skyline as you drive in. We got to our hotel, checked in and went up to our suite. I put the TV on while Bruce fought a running battle with the cockroaches in our fridge and I got my first taste of Groucho Marx hosting a re-run of *You Bet Your Life*. I felt like I'd come home. After unpacking we figured we'd head for the bar downstairs. When the elevator door opened there were two other people already inside, and we were in the magic city they happened to be Patti Smith and Leon Russell. Patti spoke -

"Are you guys over from England?"

"Yes. How did you know?" we answered.

"You look like Punk Rockers," she drawled.

1977 New York - Bruce and CP - Punk Rockers?

Bruce went to check out Sheridan Square and said he'd meet me later, Leon (I feel I can call him 'Leon', even though we never met again) wandered off to make a telephone call. And here's what I do with my chance to hang out with Patti Smith. Together we entered the bar and Patti ordered herself a Chivas Regal. Being polite, I sat a couple of stools down from her and was pathetically phased when the barman asked me what I wanted. I knew I wanted a beer, but I didn't know what particular kind they had in America and this decision was interfering with further interaction with Patti. I looked over at the only other customer in the bar, a big guy in a cowboy hat, who was sat nursing a bottle of Budweiser.

"I'll have a Budweiser, please," I asked, and attempting at small talk, I turned to her, "How's Lenny Kaye?"

"Oh do you know Lenny?"

"No", I replied, "But ...

Patti finished her drink and went off to find Leon.

I figured I'd try and engage the cowboy in a conversation.

"What's the best kind of beer here in America?" I enquired innocently.

"What?!" he snarled. "Beer's beer - What are ya? Some kind of fag!?"

Bruce's arrival in the bar probably answered his query, especially when he put his arm round me and said, "I feel quite tired now. Shall we go to bed?"

"This Is To John, From Don, Through Sean"

In 1968 I'd stood entranced at the foot of the stage in the Manchester University Student's Union and watched Captain Beefheart and The Magic Band totally destroy an audience (and me) with their unique blend of Howling Wolf vocal gymnastics and 21st century guitar playing. It was another of those moments when you knew you'd never be the same again.

A few days before, the Captain had been booked to play, of all places, Southport Floral Hall (don't laugh, I've played there myself). The audience were inside, the gear was set up, but there was no sign of the Captain or his crew. As the time drew nearer for his scheduled appearance, a very worried promoter went outside to look for any sign of them. In a van outside the gig an extremely strange bunch of people were sat in complete silence. He wandered over and enquired -

"Are you Captain Beefheart and The Magic Band?"

"We are," came the Captain's stentorian voice.

"Er, I wondered if you were going to play tonight?" asked the promoter.

"We're just checking the vibe," the Captain had replied.

Anyway, the Manchester gig was more than amazing and I felt myself glued to the spot when they'd finished. As the audience streamed out of the hall I was surprised that Beefheart himself came back on stage to pick up some bits and pieces of stage props. Somehow bravely, I called him over - "Captain, I've got both of your albums," and "Did you know that Customs and Excise had seized all the import copies of *Strictly Personal* because they thought there was acid inside the sleeves?!" With piercing eyes and leaning down at me he replied, "And they'd be correct." I gave him an Indian ring and he gave me, the enthusiastic 18 year old, a Marine Band harmonica in 'D'.

Eleven years later I couldn't believe my eyes when I again saw Beefheart, this time in the coffee bar of the rehearsal rooms we were sharing in New York. I went up to talk to him.

"Hi, Don. I bet you don't remember me?" was my opening gambit.

"Of course I do," he retorted. "How's the harmonica?"

I was just staggered. Completely stunned. I've pondered this for years. Did he give out a lot of harmonicas? Had somebody told him I was in the same building? How the hell did he know who I was. (Many years later I discovered that it was simply an ability he had. Like the way he'd know that the phone would be about to ring. A gift, whatever.) Anyway, we sat down and we talked. We talked about Roger Eagle, about Margaret Thatcher and Ronald Reagan.

"You know I predicted that they'd be elected. Back on *Troutmask Replica*." he said.

"What?" I said, ever more incredulous.

"Yeah!" he started singing, "Thatcher on a rooftop - Raygun in her hand!"

"Wow!" was my staggered response.

He had a micro-recorder around his neck and every time he said something he thought was of particular significance he'd make an aural memo to himself, always signing off with, "Copyright Don Van Vliet. 1979."

He invited me to a gig he was playing the next Saturday night, the 6th of December. It was run by two friends of mine Jane and Louis (pronounced Lewis). On 59th Street, it was called Studio 59 and it was for real music fans, the name of course a piss-take on the highly upmarket Studio 54.

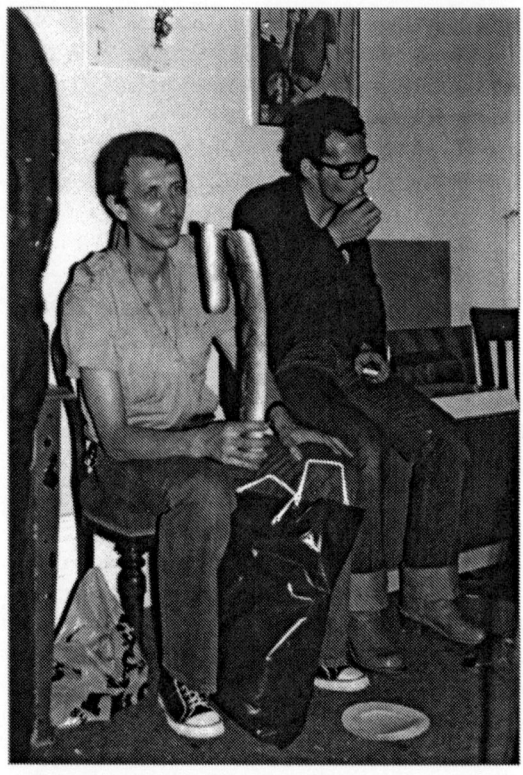

Getting the measure of Stage Manager Mel

On Friday the 5th, I was in an apartment uptown with Jimmy and Andrew and the rest of the band. We were watching the TV before going out for a drink when a newsflash came on screen. John Lennon, it said, had been shot. We sat transfixed. He'd been on the guest list for when *Sleak* opened a week later. Our office had spoken to him only a day or two earlier and now Andrew was really distraught as a reporter from the hospital stated he was dead. Andrew had known Lennon. We all felt weird, but we were able to rationalise our feelings. It was terrible he'd been murdered, but things like that happened all the time in New York and we had no idea the reaction would culminate in such an international overwhelming outpouring of grief.

Over the next week New York practically came to a standstill. Six people committed suicide, people were crying in coffee shops, bars, and clubs. A month afterwards a girl told me that she hadn't had a period 'since John died'. Excuse me! I felt that was really taking things too far. And you couldn't get a cab without the driver suddenly turning across Central Park towards the Dakota Building.

"Excuse me? Where are you going?"

"You're English. I thought you'd like to see where John Lennon died?"

"Not for an extra five bucks I don't."

So you can imagine the atmosphere the next night at Studio 59. A lot of people expected the Captain to cancel the gig, but he resisted the pressure and got on with it. The most touching moment came when he suddenly stopped the show. He hadn't mentioned Lennon at all. He 'shushed' the musicians and then held aloft a huge staff he'd been carrying. Tilting his face heavenwards he began -

"This is to John, from Don, through Sean," he incanted, his voice rumbling out of some primordial netherworld of shaman induced magick. When he finished his invocation there was a moment's silence, then the band roared into *Big Eyed Beans From Venus*, and I felt invigorated, cleansed, and in some strange way, elated.

There Are Eight Million Stories In the Naked City – Here's Another One

Ever since I'd seen an article in the *Sunday Times Colour Supplement* (1966), about the new cult of 'underground film making', I'd been fascinated by Andy Warhol. On my first trip to New York I found out where the Factory was and went and stood outside, soaking up some of the vibes as Beefheart did at Southport. No-one came to enquire what I was doing, and it wasn't until 1979 that I finally got to meet the man himself.

Kim and Branca from *Soho News*, got invited to all the best parties in Manhattan and one day they asked me if I'd like to go to one of Andy's 'do's'. I didn't need asking twice. It was a big affair being held at the Palladium, an old ballroom somewhere in mid-town that had re-invented itself as a Rock venue. I'd been there the year before, with Buzzcocks when in the dressing room after the show I was talking to Pete Shelley. A groupie came up and asked him who I was.

"He's my uncle," Pete had replied in a deadpan accent.

"Eughh! That's so gross!" she grimaced, before moving away.

I'm still uncle to Pete.

Anyway, the Warhol story. I found myself there attending one of Warhol's periodic attempts to relaunch his cable TV show and couldn't believe how crowded the Palladium was. Kim and Branca kept pointing people out to me –

US flyer for Sleak

"Oh, Look. There's Robert De Niro. Isn't he with Dustin?" they'd say.

My neck began hurting from straining to see people.

"Oh, there's Liza, and is that Bianca?"

They could tell I was getting celebbed out.

"Come on," said Kim. "I'll introduce you to Andy. He'll be thrilled to meet you."

She began to drag me across the ballroom floor towards a knot of people surrounding Andy. Suddenly I was face to face with the man himself.

"Andy, this is CP ..." began Kim. Warhol looked about as interested as if she's offered him a glass of water. "... He's got a show opening soon."

His eyes suddenly lit up and he took my hand. "Oh, I'm so pleased to meet you. Where are you from?" came his New York Warhol drawl.

"Manchester ... England," I answered.

"Isn't that cute?" he told nobody in particular. "Here, let me take your photo." He produced a Polaroid camera from nowhere and a quick flash told me he'd done just that. "Now, is there anything you'd like?"

It was two in the morning, I was fairly high, a tad overexcited at meeting

Warhol, and couldn't think of a single thing.

Kim came to my rescue - "He'd like English muffins and tea," she said.

"English muffins and tea?" repeated Warhol, like it was the most exotic thing he'd ever heard of. "Okay" he said.

All this time Andy was accompanied by several smartly-suited young men, one of whom strode off as soon as Kim had spoken. Andy turned to talk to somebody else and we wandered off to do some more star gazing.

Twenty minutes later, I don't know how they did it, but this was New York after all, his 'young man' walked up to us and handed us a take-away bag containing tea and English muffins.

I was very impressed.

The Raspberry Ripple

It was a week of shows, in different cinemas around London, in the week before Christmas 1978. We were Ian Dury's 'special guests' and the incessant partying was taking its toll. Being based in London for a whole week meant that each day we were off enjoying ourselves in the fleshpots of the city, visiting museums and art galleries and such like. Strangely, when we each individually returned from our cultural forays into the seething metropolis, ready to take the stage and perform for the good people of London we appeared to be intoxicated with the delight of it all. Then there was the back stage hospitality, the likes of which had seldom been seen since the hey-day of the Roman Empire. Tables groaned under the weight of crates of fine ale and chicken legs, paper party hats were strewn everywhere and then there were the mirrors all lined up with razor blades on them ready for action.

When we'd first signed to Blackhill we'd never heard of 'riders'. We quickly discovered that these were the backstage

GM Ian Dury

provisions for the band, attached to the contract that was sent by the band's management to the promoter. The excesses of some Rock stars' riders had become legendary. Rod Stewart, for instance, insisted on Chablis being kept in an ice-bucket at the side of the stage, and Cat Stevens on a kitchen being available in the dressing room for the use of his Indian chef. Kevin Ayer's rider looked like a list of the contents of an Oddbins wine merchants. Not to be outdone when we realised that this was a perk of the job, the Berts had drawn up a rider demanding current issues of *The Dandy* and *The Beano*, and four boxes of Brillo pads. I'll never forget one social secretary at one gig apologising to us over and over again that he couldn't find the latest issues of the kid's comics anywhere and would we still go on?

GM Ged Murray Ace Photographer and CP taking five (and anything else they can get)

Meanwhile, we're at this one gig at the Lewisham Odeon, and an already 'merry' Albertos were busily wrapping their laughing tackle round as many bottle necks as possible before going on stage. There might also have been a certain amount of nasal carnage going on. The result was that the following morning in the Blackhill office we stood rather shamefacedly in front of Ian and his personal roady, Spider. In order to appreciate fully the following conversation, please bear in mind the Spider was a former associate of the Krays.

"What you lot done last night was a fuckin' disgrace," he started, glancing over at Ian who was sat shaking his head in agreement.

"You let yourselves down and worse of all you let Ian down. Ain't that right Ian?"

"You let me down boys," Ian replied, twiddling his cane.

I had a dim memory of Norman Watt Roy and the other Blockheads being as pissed as we'd been.

"And before you mention the Blockheads ..." Spider rampaged on menacingly, "... they've been dealt with – if you catch my drift."

We did and suitably hung our heads even lower.

"If I catch you having so much as a small glass of sherry before tonight's show, do you know what I'm going to do with you?"

Les sniggered like a schoolboy. Not a smart move given the circumstances. Spider grabbed him by the throat and held him against a wall.

"I'm going to stick my fingers up my arse and then shove 'em down your throats until you puke that evil alcohol out of your systems! Am I making myself clear?"

We all decided to nod in agreement.

That night we just stuck to drugs, but there was another calamity, this time not of our making.

There were big 'No Admittance' and 'Danger' signs all around the orchestra pit. The reason for this was because we'd filled the pit with 'confetti bombs'. These were huge cardboard cylinders packed with confetti on top of very large explosive charges ready for when, at the climax of the show, they'd be let off and with an almighty bang the audience would be showered with tiny bits of paper.

NME photographer, Jill Furmanovsky had done what all photographers do when they see a sign that says, 'No Admittance', totally ignored it and gone into the pit. We were singing away as our show came to its climax and the bombs went off. She left the pit then. Well, she went upwards out of the pit, if you see what I mean. About twelve feet or so into the air. And then she went back down again. Turned out she'd been standing on one of them to get a better shot.

Blackhill sent flowers and a crate of champagne to her in hospital on our behalf.

When An Old Cricketer Leaves The Crease

Despite everything we did to put them off, The Pink Floyd seemed determined to like us. Even when we beat them at cricket. It was one of the great unsung sporting triumphs of 1975, a one-day event that took place in middle England on a sultry day in midsummer. Whether the match was designed to give them some street cred, or ensure that for at least one day we might eat well, it's hard to say, but Andrew and Peter were quite excited and so we set off bright and early in the Bertmobile one morning and headed for a small local ground the Floyd had hired for the occasion. We knew we were there when our clapped out Transit van gave a derisory cough as it spied a herd of Range Rovers grazing peacefully next to a marquee that had been specially erected for the occasion.

JB Jimmy and CP in harmony

The Pink Floyd and their exotic womenfolk were laid out on sun-loungers, dressed impeccably in cricketing whites. I think the guys from Hipgnosis and some other rich people, made up the rest of their team. We piled out of the van in an Oxfam assortment of differing garb. Roy Harper, who was acting as umpire for the day, looked at our motley outfits and tutted. The tutting became a slightly raised hub-bub as I decamped and began erecting a small tent that was (not) going to act as the Berts pavilion, but as, the cardboard sign stuck on the front of it proclaimed - 'Syd's Bad Trip Tent'.

But they took it in their stride by humiliating us further by offering Pimms and canapés. I thought they said 'cannabis' and this led to even more tutting. The match began and we went in first. I declined the offer of batting, preferring to stay in the tent and communing with nature. It had been agreed that my part in the match would be that of 'witchdoctor', I was to emerge every now and then wearing beads and necklaces, shriek from the sidelines and put spells on them. My secret 'magickal weapon' for the second half was an old mole trap, that I kept casually dropping on the pitch near wherever one of them looked like running. Roy Harper told me not to be so stupid, so, like Achilles, I took to my tent and sulked.

Our real 'secret weapon' and the one who won the match for us was our roady, Black Paul Young. Paul was West Indian in origin and took his cricket seriously. He played barefoot which unnerved the Pink Floyd even more. At lunch they tried to nobble him with a large barrel of real ale that they'd laid on, but we saved him from humiliation by drinking most of it before he could.

At the end of the day there was an undignified argument about which team won and unfortunate accusations of the umpire's bias were subsequently reported in the popular musical press of the period. It was suggested that the Pink Floyd's win was the result of Roy Harper's flagrant favouritism. At least that's what we told everybody. Yet even this scandal didn't put the Floyd off liking us and over the years they watched our career closely.

CP, This Is BP

Sometimes it felt that the more abusive about other musicians we were, the more they wanted to be 'friends'. A journalist once told me that one successful group he'd interviewed had reckoned that if the Berts hadn't taken the piss out of you then you couldn't be that successful. People actually sent us their latest albums (are you still out there Budgie). Virgin got very excited when we asked for some copies of Mike Oldfield's *Tubular Bells* and asked when we were going to do a parody. We weren't – we just used to burn the albums on stage.

Robert Plant tried to be matey once, but got put off because Tony Bowers actually thought he was joking when he introduced himself. Tony kept saying – "Hey lads. There's some idiot here who keeps saying his name's Rubber Plant!"

As we got higher up the totem pole we cherished the opportunity to help new bands and whenever we could we put groups that were just starting out as support on our tours. If they were support at somewhere like the Marquee we'd ensure they got paid more than the £5 we'd got when we started out. The problem with all these altruistic acts was that the support bands we had seemed to get a lot bigger than us. Devo for example. The Stranglers. The Police. Now there were a bunch of guys who took to touring with the Berts. The climax of our show at that time was a raucous, off key version of Cliff Richards' *Summer Holiday*. We couldn't keep Sting, Andy and Stewart from racing onstage and joining in. We tried making them annoyed by send ups of their numbers revolving round the concept of food – *I Can't Stand Losing You* became *I Can't Stand Lasagne*, *Roxanne* was *Rocksalmon*, *So Lonely* was *Salami*, etc. Les had even tried to piss Ian Dury off with a version of *Sex and Drugs and Rock and Roll* which became mutated into *Eggs and Chips and Sausage Roll*. It was no use though, everybody thought it was hilarious, especially the people who'd written them.

Led Zeppelin's publicist at the time was a wonderful Irishman named BP Fallon and I'll never forget the first time I met him. Sometimes the Bers would sleep under the table at Blackhill. One morning, bright and early as we rose, a muffled grunting noise came from beside our sleeping bags. A small crumpled figure dragged himself upright into a sitting position. He wasn't one of us. Somehow he must have become attached to us in the night, though none of us could remember it. He introduced himself as BP Fallon and then casually tossed an address book to Jimmy.

"Could you pick a name out of there for me, please," he asked politely. "Any one'll do."

Jimmy read out a number and BP reached for the phone and dialled.

"Mick? Yeah, Mick. It's BP. I'd just like to apologise for last night. See you around."

As he put the phone down he explained –

"I always get so pissed the night before that I can never remember who I was with. All I know is I must have insulted somebody, so every morning I pick a name at random and phone up and tell them how sorry I am. Usually works."

This is how I came to know one of the world's greatest Irishmen. Bernard Patrick Fallon, PR consultant to the stars.

When Bob Dylan came to town in 1978 it was inevitable that he and BP would hook up. Dylan was doing a lot of socialising and visiting gigs along with assorted Rockeratti and hangers on, which is how it came to pass one night when we were performing at the Electric Circus in Camden and BP came excitedly to the side of the stage while we were playing and gestured me over, "CP! He's here! I've got Dylan here. He's come to see you play."

This was too much. I was so excited I could have done a cartwheel. Then a cold wave of fear washed over me. What do you do in circumstances like this? Out of all the people in the universe Dylan was the only one in front of whom I'd be utterly tongue-tied. There was nothing I could think of to say - But wait! Yes there was. When the number ended I grabbed the mike from a surprised looking Jimmy who was about to deliver a very carefully rehearsed ad-lib.

"Ladies and gentlemen ..." I began, "... We'd like to do a number now by Bob Dylan, but he never plays any of our stuff, so fuck him!" And off we went into *Teenage Paradise*, or whatever.

For some reason Dylan took umbrage at my light-hearted quip and off he and his entourage went to Dingwalls to watch Link Wray.

JB U-Boat Pasta-Man Vibrations!

11

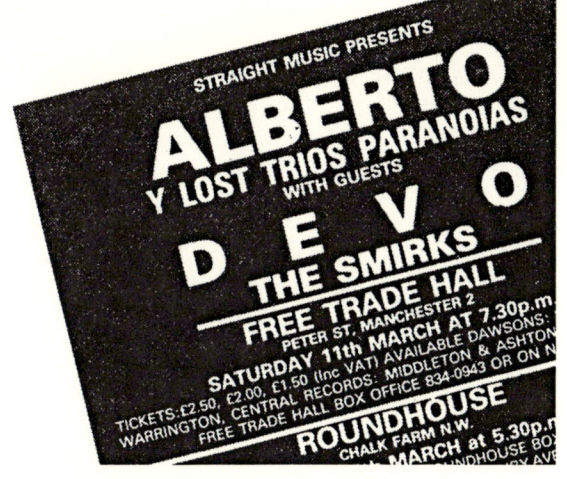

CHAPTER ELEVEN
THE CURSE OF THE BERTS

STRAIGHT MUSIC PRESENTS

ALBERTO Y LOST TRIOS PARANOIAS
WITH GUESTS
DEVO
THE SMIRKS

FREE TRADE HALL
PETER ST, MANCHESTER 2
SATURDAY 11th MARCH at 7.30p.m.
TICKETS: £2.50, £2.00, £1.50 (Inc VAT) AVAILABLE DAWSONS:
WARRINGTON, CENTRAL RECORDS: MIDDLETON & ASHTON
FREE TRADE HALL BOX OFFICE 834-0943 OR ON N

ROUNDHOUSE
CHALK FARM N.W.
MARCH at 5.30p.m.

Ten years of sitting in a van. Ten years of driving thousands of miles in order to insult other musicians. And for all the good it did in the long run we may as well have stayed at home. By the time the New Romantics appeared it was obvious that there was no point in going on any longer, Rock was doing a pretty good job of sending itself up without our help. And maybe we were taking ourselves too seriously too.

We'd had a good crack at it, but, as various people said, we were either too far ahead of our time, too stoned, too drunk, too paranoid, or even, too funny. There was a fair bit of sheer bad luck attendant on our endeavours as well – We used to call it – The Curse of The Berts!

Wit's end

THE Albertos had just played their first gig at the Marquee; it was the summer of 1974. Les Prior was in the bar attempting to fill me in on all the usual details. We had a drink, I offered him a cigarette.

"No thanks," he said. "I'm dying of cancer."

The joke was stinging, mirthless. Les Prior *was* dying of cancer. Last month, it finally killed him. He died in Manchester, early on the morning of January 31.

He had known since 1973 that he was suffering from Hodgkinson's Disease, a cancer of the lymph glands. He also knew that his condition was probably terminal. At first it didn't prevent him from appearing regularly with the Albertos. In fact, his wild, improvised links between the group's musical parodies usually gave the Albertos' act its only true satiric edge.

Inevitably, as his illness became more severe, he was forced to retire from constant touring. During the last years of his life he appeared irregularly with the group. However, when he appeared as the deejay in the Albertos' musical "Sleak!" at the Royal Court, it was clear that his wit was as sharp and inventive as ever. I also remember being reduced to tears of laughter when he compered the first Stiff tour.

In the unreleased movie shot during that epic trek, he provides one of the hilarious highlights. He is backstage at one of the gigs with Nick Lowe. Basher is strumming away at an acoustic guitar, playing "Blowin' In The Wind". Les is playing a rock critic, analysing every line of the song. "I see — what you're talking about here is a *metaphorical* blowing in the wind situation . . . "

It's funny. Everybody knew he was going to die, but I don't think anyone actually expected him to go ahead and *do* it. — ALLAN JONES.

Don't Touch That Dial!

Take television – Please! Take television! – Thanks to Tony Wilson we had some presence on British TV. We appeared on our local Granada network *What's On* in the mid 1970s and then on the nationally networked, *So It Goes*. One memorable occasion featured me playing a dub version of the Beatles' *Strawberry Fields Forever* on Albie Donnelly's (of Supercharge fame) bald head, something I'd wanted to do ever since I first thought of it.

But getting on the BBC was another matter altogether. Their flagship Rock show was *The Old Grey Whistle Test*, a programme that we detested because of its apparent reluctance to feature any group that wasn't American. Fronted by the snake-like hissing sibilance of 'Whispering' Bob Harris, *Whistle Test* was shot on top of an ancient Red Indian burial ground on a set littered with the bloated corpses of coke-addled buffoons in velvet trousers whose bodies should have been hung upside-down in public lavatories as a warning against VD. Or maybe I'm thinking of another programme? Anyway, they wouldn't have us on.

You can imagine our surprise therefore, when BBC2 approached us about doing a *Sight and Sound In Concert*. This was a TV and stereo radio simulcast that went out on a Saturday evening at 6.30 pm. As it was also broadcast live we promised to behave and we were duly booked.

We went on and did a truncated, cleaned up version of our set - or so we thought. The BBC received the most complaints they'd ever had for a single programme, a record I believe we held for quite a few years. The phones had started ringing when Jimmy started singing *Old Trust*, our dog song. Some guy complained that his children's pet dog had been run over that afternoon and it was in appalling taste and why weren't the BBC more sensitive about what they broadcast. Jimmy then brought Bob on for *Anadin*, and he did his usual 'throwing up' gag at the beginning of the number, and then Jimmy carried on his great big spoon of 'coke' for Tony to snort. Apparently a lot of families around the British Isles were having their dinner at that time of the evening and were rather put off by Bob spewing into the camera (oddly, none of the complainants mentioned the 'coke'!). Then Les had frightened some children by his appearance. Well, that was fair enough, he sometimes frightened us, but this was television - we thought Bruce Forsyth looked pretty freaky, but we never complained about it!

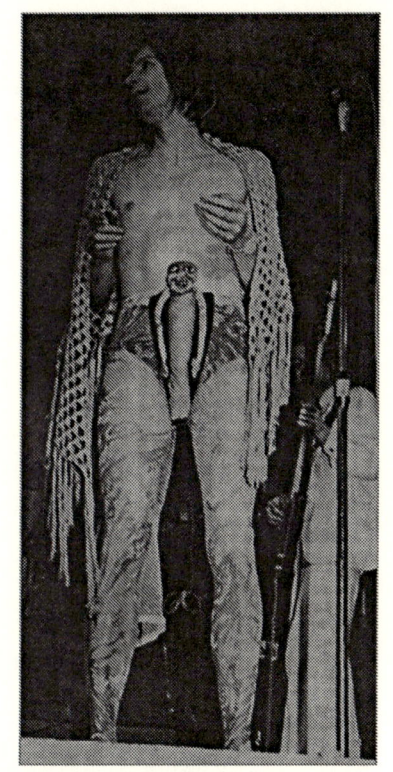

Les and his codpiece Henry

Then some viewers found the Rastaman introduction to *Where Have All The Flowers Gone*, "There will be Birmingham and Luton tonight!" racist stereotyping. I'd been worried about that too and we'd dropped it until both Aswad and Burning Spear had asked why. They thought it was hilarious and so we put it back in.

The ka ka really hit the air-conditioning with the final number *Gobbin' on Life*. We were slightly overrunning at this point and what we didn't know was that the producer started rolling the final credits just as the instrumental break happened. He ordered the engineer to fade to black and then sat back to watch as Jimmy plunged a large knife into his chest. A torrent of blood gushed out of him as he collapsed on the floor. Behind him, Bruce triumphantly led the band into the final chorus using a pair of gigantic wooden crucifixes as drum sticks, holding them aloft as the final note died away.

The thing was, the engineer had disobeyed his order to fade out the programme. He'd let the credits roll and then carried on broadcasting the show. The stunned nation had just witnessed a particularly messy suicide accompanied by heretical and blasphemous idolatry. It was then that the phones started really ringing. I have since been told that the particular engineer 'left' the BBC shortly afterwards.

That seemed to be the end of our TV career, as far as it went anyway, in this country at least. It wasn't until 1981 that we got another chance.

Teach Yourself Gibberish

Disco Werewolf - The children's tea-time treat

The Curse of the Berts 209

Granada rang - would we like to do a comedy series? - It wasn't Tony this time, but a producer called Diana Bramwell. I went to the obligatory 'developmental lunch', and she outlined what she had in mind. A seven-part, late-night series of shows, aimed at an adult audience. She'd seen us doing *Never Mind The Bullocks*, and thought there was enough scope within the Berts for a challenging and different kind of TV comedy.

What I came up with was that each show would consist of a series of sketches, linked by a theme. The themes were based on letters of the alphabet, 'P' for Pop, for instance. 'K' for lying. We shot the pilot and then waited. And then we waited some more. I'm constantly amazed that anything ever gets made for television, so much time is spent waiting. Finally word came – the show was go!

CP decoding DaVinci's macroproposition of the Fabula inherent within the metatext, aka Gibberish

We filmed it at the same time as Sir Lawrence Olivier was shooting his Shakespeare season for Granada, and there was much confusion in the make-up departments as we wandered in and out dressed in a variety of strange costumes and so did he and his troupe. One day he followed us into our studio thinking we were the cast of *King Lear*.

When the seven episodes were shot, edited and in the can, we prepared for what was to turn out to be our final tour of the UK, though we didn't know it then. Next, Granada rang and told us there'd been a change of plan. Instead of a seven-part, late-night comedy series, the whole thing was to be cut down to six shows and broadcast during children's hour. I pointed out that they were thematic, you couldn't edit them in and out, they wouldn't make sense. I huffed and puffed, blustered and harangued, all to no avail. There we were, the wild men of Rock, the Godfather's of Punk, the blasphemous spawn of Satan, going out during children's hour after Sooty and Sweep. It was madness!

JB Jimmy Hibbert having a great Knight

Before the series was due for transmission they contracted me to write seven more, which I did. Then they rang up and told me they weren't going to make them after all. It became apparent that somebody at Granada, somebody very high up, had something against the Berts. Several years afterwards, this person was approached by Channel 4 asking if they could reshow *Teach Yourself Gibberish*. They were told that it would be 'over his dead body'. One day I'd like to arrange that (the reshowing, of course).

And so, as MTV came on air and the world entered the video age, the Albertos found themselves thwarted and stood on the dock watching the ship sail into the distance. And that's why you never see clips of us on any of those television shows with names like 'I Remember The 1970s'.

Heads Down No Nonsense Mindless Boogie

Another example of the 'Curse Of The Berts' is the trouble we had with our one single to get in the charts, *Heads Down No Nonsense Mindless Boogie*. Shamelessly promoted with a free, give-away single of a wonderful little ditty entitled *Fuck You*, our homage to headbangers everywhere was actually 'record of the week' on one Radio One show despite a barrage of negative press criticism from the tabloids. For the umpteenth time in our career we found ourselves being slammed by *The News of the World*, with a 'Must we fling this filth at our kids!' banner headline.

On the 23rd of September 1978 we officially entered the charts at number 28 and were put on standby for *Top Of The Pops*. That Wednesday night we sat in Blackhill waiting for official confirmation that we were going to appear on the next day's programme. It never came and we were never told why. We were the highest new entry of anybody that week, but I guess somebody at the Beeb had it in for us as well.

"Dead! What Do You Mean, Dead?!"

We'd got to New York. The Police (the group, that is), The Clash and The Pink Floyd, had put ten thousand quid each into getting us over there so we could do *Sleak* off Broadway. There was absolutely no reason why it shouldn't emulate the success of its British run. But then everybody had forgotten, cue thunder, 'The Curse Of The Berts' –

John Lennon was shot a week after we opened and, being as how the subject matter of *Sleak* was about assassination, death and Rock music, it seemed politic to put the show on hold for a little while. The enforced interim meant that our budget was stretched further, but we gritted our teeth and kept our fingers crossed.

US program for Sleak

Sting and I did a few radio ads to try and keep the show in people's minds and then I had a brainwave. I persuaded Andrew to let me make one more – It was quite short and featured only me doing my best John Lennon impersonation. It went like this –

"Hi, my name's John Lennon and if I were alive today I'd go and see Alberto Y Lost Trios Paranoias in *Sleak* …"

It got broadcast a couple of times before it was lifted off air. I got a few death threats, nothing much, but the atmosphere of New York was too down for 'a light-hearted look at death'. Not a lot of people were going out that winter and we decided to keep the show on hold under things got more settled down. I'm still waiting, as, I believe, so are The Police, The Clash and The Pink Floyd. Now, where did I put that thirty thousand????

Treading The Boards

As I've already shown how I turned down the chance to keep *Sleak* running without us, I won't go on about it again, but instead go on about how its follow-ups *Never Mind The Bullocks* and *Skite* fell apart.

JB Never Mind The Bullocks Ensemble

Bullocks was supposed to be 'a light-hearted look at the Black Death' and was co-written with comic John Dowie. Basically it was a costume farce with absolutely no pretensions to artistic integrity, far from it. It was simply a knockabout romp. When we played it in the North of England it went down fine, but when we opened in London the knives were out. Sharing the same stage as the *Sooty and Sweep Show* probably didn't help. Fortunately, Matthew Corbett and his puppets were on in the afternoon and we were on in the evening, so there was only marginal overlap, but all in all, through a combination of bad decisions on our part and a genuine desire by the London press to stick the boot in on anything that was regional, *Bullocks* was led to the abattoir after only three weeks.

Skite was never given the chance to be panned, because it never got produced. Peter Cook was all set to come in and direct it and we had a few meetings to make changes to the script, but we went over to New York to lose everybody's money on *Sleak* instead. RIP.

We've Had Great Fun Playing For You

Our last official gig was in Tel Aviv, our last unofficial one at the Lamplight Club in Chorlton-cum-Hardy in Manchester. We'd reached the dizzying heights of the top of Division 2. We were amongst the highest paid live acts in the country (bear in mind, not that many people were touring then), but the joke had worn too thin. All the pressure of writing and performing had left me so strung out you could have hung washing from me. Jimmy had made a solo Heavy Metal album, *Mister Wonderful*. Bruce had found a more lucrative career playing drums with Vinnie Reilly in the Durutti Column. The Berts just drifted apart. You could say we called

---

OBITUARY

LES PRIOR: an appreciation by C. P. Lee

LES PRIOR, who died peacefully at home on January 31, was an integral part of Alberto Y Los Trios Paranoias. We called him factor X, because you never knew from one minute to the next what outrage he was going to commit, not only on the audience, but also on the band. This was the key to his uniqueness, the blend of devastating verbal wit and tightrope walking bravado that endeared him to so many artists and audiences, not only with the Albertos, but as MC with the Stiff tours.

The instrument that Les played was the crowd, and on a good night he played it like a master. His freewheeling, improvisational verbalising made him one of Britain's best comedians, but by choosing to work within a rock setting his talent remained sadly unrecognised by the public at large.

Perhaps his peak came when he played the DJ in *Sleak*. This part gave free rein to his mischievous sense of the bizarre and rapidly developed into a show within a show. Here he developed a barrage of puns and gags that epitomised the sleazy world of the 'all purpose club': "Don't forget, Wednesday night is heavy night — come down and drink some cement . . . Here's one by Bob Marley and the Marleytiles, called 'Whisky In My Jah' . . . It's the Pink Freud — 'See Emily Play With Herself'."

All this was performed whilst Les battled with a turntable that possessed the capabilities of a British army mortar, hurling records and Les in the air with breakneck ferocity.

Translating any humour onto vinyl is tricky and translating Les's was trickier, but if needs be he could turn out funny tracks, made even funnier by his strangled vocals. On stage there were times when we never reached the end of the song because we were doubled up in hysterics at his singing. 'Pavlov's Dog' became his tour de force and all the time Les was well enough to perform we never dropped it from the set.

Les joined the Albertos on our third gig. He already knew he had cancer and that his time was limited. This was a contributory factor to his attitude to performing — he had nothing to lose and this gave his style an edge that he continually hurled himself over. Sometimes he'd fly and sometimes he'd fall, but whatever the outcome it was always a uniquely Les performance.

Despite his rapidly deteriorating condition Les never once complained, and when the end came it was a release for him and a loss for all of us. But for his friends who love him and for all the people who saw him in action he's left a legacy in our hearts that will never fade, because the gift he gave us his greatest gift — that of laughter.

Pic: Chalkie Davies

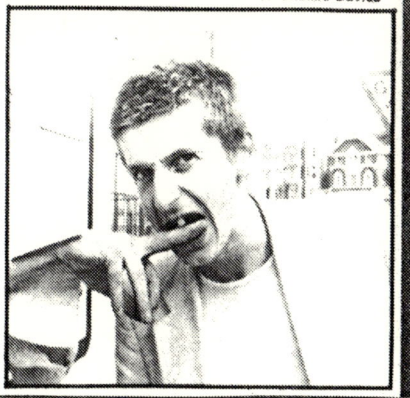

it a day due to musical indifference, whatever. The gig was up. Bruce always used to tell me about a recurring dream that he had. There was a furious knocking on the door. When we opened it a bunch of policemen were stood there. "Alright, lads," they said. "The game's up. Did you think you could get away with this crap forever?"

We made a lot of mistakes and we did a lot of things right. Maybe the fact that we never actually set out to 'make it' affected some of our 'career' decisions. I don't know. Maybe we had insufficient financial backing to create better shows, or we had lousy record deals, or maybe the management was inept, or perhaps I was too idealistic. Whatever, I wouldn't have had it any other way and the older I get the more convinced I become that talent has got nothing to do with 'success' in the music biz. A couple of years after the Berts' demise I got a shot producing an album for a friend of mine who was one of the hottest actors in the country at the time, Tom Watt. Tom was 'Lofty' in the *EastEnders* TV soap and was watched regularly by around 18 million people a week. John Scott and I made an album with him, featuring Josie Lawrence on a couple of duets and a whole heap of talented session people doing the backing. There was quite a lot of media interest in the single, a Cockney Rap version of Dylan's *Subterranean Homesick Blues*. The video (now on youtube.com) which features members of The Fall and Joy Division as well as Tom, John and me was shown on a couple of TV shows. But when the singles arrived from the plant they were warped and had to be junked. By the time the replacements arrived the buzz had gone and I thought to myself, if I couldn't make it in music with this kind of publicity and pedigree of players, it was time to give up. So I did ... though the Salford Sheiks might disagree ...

> *Chris Lee has proved himself ... illustrious*
> *Through constant industry ... industrious*
> *So What?*
> *Could you be calm and placid if you were full of*
> *Lysergic Acid?*
>
> BRUCE MITCHELL

see more at www.itsahotun.com/wwwt

When we were thin ... RIP Mongo (2007)

Alberto Y Lost Trios Paranoias

ALBERTOLISTOGRAPHY

SINGLES
Dread Jaws (Transatlantic) 1975
Old Trust (Logo) 1976
Heads Down, No Nonsense, Mindless Boogie (Logo) 1978
Crusin' With Santa (New Hormones) 1981

EP
Snuff Rock (Stiff) 1977

ALBUMS
Alberto Y Lost Trios Paranoias (Transatlantic) 1975
Italians From Outer Space (Logo) 1976
Skite (Logo) 1978
Worst of the Berts (Logo) 1981

CDs
Snuff Rock (Demon/MauMau) 1991
Radio Sweat (Overgound) 1996
Alberto Y Lost Trios Paranoias (Sanctuary) 2003

VISUALS
Sight and Sound (BBC) 1977 and Teach Yourself Gibberish (Granada) 1981- not commercially available ... However, there is a growing Berts' presence on the Internet due to the conjunction of Pisces in Uranus. This will have moved away in the morning to leave a few damp patches here and there. In the meantime you might like to follow these links:

www.youtube.com
To see moving images of the Berts (all of them in colour!) you can go to this site, search Alberto Y Lost Trios Paranoias or SNUFF ROCK and be taken back in time just like that!

www.cplee.co.uk
With its shrine to the Berts, visitors can marvel at a variety of wondrous sights. The site also has a few audio tracks to play with and a 'What's On' (Gig Info) page.

OTHER BOOKS BY CP LEE

Like The Night (Revisited)
2004

Helter Skelter Publishing (United Kingdom)
ISBN 1-900924331 (2nd revised edition)
Paperback - 224 Pages

CP Lee's eyewitness account of Dylan's pivotal 1966 show at the Manchester Free Trade Hall brings to life the controversial time when Dylan turned his back on folk music in favour of rock 'n' roll which culminated at the Manchester show where a fan shouted 'Judas' at Dylan for his perceived betrayal

Shake, Rattle and Rain
2002

Hardinge Simpole Limited (United Kingdom)
ISBN 1-9781843820499
Paperback - 336 Pages

Combining oral history and personal observation, this book provides an invaluable insight into what has made Manchester such an innovative creative music centre over the last five decades - from Beat clubs to the Hacienda, from Music Force to Factory Records, the Summer of Love and beyond.

Like A Bullet of Light - The Films of Bob Dylan
2000

Helter Skelter Publishing (United Kingdom)
ISBN 1-9781900924061
Paperback - 192 Pages

An in-depth study of an often overlooked part of Dylan's oeuvre, this is CP Lee's compelling portrait of an enigmatic artist as keen to challenge perceptions in the visual medium as he is in his better-known career in music.

Orders/Enquiries about CP Lee's books

books@itsahotun.com

1972 - Scruff

Hotun Press

Printed in the United Kingdom
by Lightning Source UK Ltd.
123187UK00002B/64-999/A